D1554488

The Depletion Myth

Sherry H. Olson

The Depletion Myth

A History of Railroad Use of Timber

Harvard University Press, Cambridge, Massachusetts, 1971

This study was based largely on publications of the railway engineering societies, the Association of American Railroads, and the U.S. Forest Service. Most were available at the Harvard Forest, Petersham, Massachusetts, and the library of the Bureau of Railway Economics, Washington, D.C. Published documents of the nineteenth century were found in the Widener Library, Harvard University; the Lloyd Library, Cincinnati; and the Peabody Library, Baltimore.

The cooperation of the Burlington Lines made possible the more detailed study of one large railroad system. In early 1970 the Burlington became part of the Burlington Northern, Inc., through merger with the Northern Pacific and the Great Northern. I would like to acknowledge the help of Richard C. Overton of the University of Western Ontario, historian of the Burlington; the late Julius J. Alms, vice-president; and H. V. Schiltz, director of purchases, who arranged for the cooperation of the railroad. I would especially like to thank Carl Swanson, purchasing agent; C. S. Morton, superintendent of timber preservation, his assistant Mr. Johnson and his predecessor, Harry Duncan of Galesburg, Illinois; E. J. Brown, chief engineer, his assistant, L. R. Hall, and Mr. Davidson, bridge engineer. All of them opened their records and contributed generously from their knowledge. Their data were supplemented for the nineteenth century from the Burlington Archives, maintained in the Newberry Library, Chicago.

Others who were helpful in providing manuscript data and knowledge from their experience were George M. Hunt, former director of the Forest Products Laboratory, Madison, Wisconsin; Donald G. Coleman in charge of public relations at the Forest Products Laboratory; J. C. McClellan, chief forester for the American Forest Products Industries, Inc., Washington, D.C.; J. Elmer Monroe, director, and Kenneth Hurdle, statistician, the Bureau of Railway Economics; Paul D. Brentlinger, forester of the Pennsylvania Railroad, Philadelphia; F. F. Wangaard, of Colorado State University; Ernest M. Gould, Jr., at the Harvard Forest; Elwood R. Maunder, director of the Forest History Society, Santa Cruz, and Joseph A. Miller, at Yale University.

None of these people should be held responsible for my interpretation of their records or of events in which they took part.

A John E. Rovensky Fellowship from the Lincoln Educational Foundation, 1963–1964, made the study possible. I want to thank members of the geography department of the Johns Hopkins University—Hugh Raup, David A. Bramhall, and M. Gordon Wolman—for their encouragement and help. I also appreciate the indulgence of the librarians of the Johns Hopkins University. Maps and graphs were prepared by Robert E. Winter.

A peculiar responsibility must be attributed to my great-grandfather, John Pinkney Brown, the "Johnny Catalpa-Seed" of the railroads and author and publisher of *Practical Arboriculture* (Connersville, Indiana, 1906). I owe him an apology for finding that catalpa plantations were uneconomic investments for railroads. But the railroads found out fifty years ago, and Grandpa Brown did manage to transmit to the third and fourth generations his enthusiasm for trees, railroads, and the making of books.

The greatest credit is due John C. Goodlett, much of whose research and writing lie unfinished because of the time he shared with his students and colleagues, the standard of craftsmanship he demanded of them and of himself, and a life so generous, so intense and brimming over, that it called for more years than were given.

Sherry H. Olson

Contents

Illustrations

Figures

Source: Franklin B. Hough, "Report on Kinds and Quantities of Timber Used for Railroad Ties," in U.S. Department of Agriculture, *Report on Forestry*, IV (1884).

Source: Franklin B. Hough, "Report on Kinds and Quantities of Timber Used for Railroad Ties," in U.S. Department of Agriculture, *Report on Forestry*, IV (1884).

Source: Franklin B. Hough, "Report on Kinds and Quantities of Timber Used for Railroad Ties," in U.S. Department of Agriculture, *Report on Forestry*, IV (1884).

Source: E. N. Munns, "The Distribution of Important Forest Trees of the United States," U.S. Department of Agriculture, *Miscellaneous Publication* (No. 287, 1938).

Source: E. N. Munns, "The Distribution of Important Forest Trees of the United States," U.S. Department of Agriculture, *Miscellaneous Publication* (No. 287, 1938).

Source: E. N. Munns, "The Distribution of Important Forest Trees of the United States," U.S. Department of Agriculture, *Miscellaneous Publication* (No. 287, 1938).

Figures

Source: E. N. Munns, "The Distribution of Important Forest Trees of the United States," U.S. Department of Agriculture, *Miscellaneous Publication* (No. 287, 1938).

Sources: Outlays in dollars per mile for rail, ties, track labor, and rail prices are three-year averages derived from MS storekeepers' accounts and rail records in the Burlington Archives, Newberry Library, Chicago. All figures are given in current dollars, not deflated. Crosstie prices are from Burlington reports to state railroad commissions of Illinois, Iowa, Kansas, and Nebraska, and from construction accounts (MS) in the Burlington Archives. Figures after 1894 refer only to lines west, where ties are higher in price than on lines east (in Illinois and Iowa). Variance of figures for the 1880s is explained by the broader geographic range. Larger outlay for ties after 1899 was probably the result of added costs for preservative treatment. Tie renewals per mile of road, as reported to the Illinois Railroad Commission, are higher than renewals per mile of all track, as "road" included the main track only. The Burlington had about 50 percent more track in branches and sidings, not maintained to the same quality.

Source: E. N. Munns, "The Distribution of Important Forest Trees of the United States," U.S. Department of Agriculture, *Miscellaneous Publication* (No. 287, 1938).

Photographs of a timber trestle in Washington show the structural members, including a timber bulkhead (less common now than formerly), the creosote-treated cloth placed over the ends of the piles, and the heart center timbers used for caps.

Sources: For railroad plantations, from Table 2; for species ranges, E. N. Munns, "The Distribution of Important Forest Trees of the United States," U.S. Department of Agriculture, *Miscellaneous Publication* (No. 287, 1938).

Source: Handbook on Wood Preservation (Baltimore: American Wood-Preservers' Association, 1916).

Source: U.S. Department of Agriculture, Forest Service, in cooperation with the American Wood-Preservers' Association, *Wood Preservation Statistics,* published annually since 1909 in *Proceedings,* American Wood-Preservers' Association, and as a printed separate.

Sources: U.S. Department of Agriculture, Forest Service, in cooperation with the American Wood-Preservers' Association, *Wood Preservation Statistics.* Crosstie renewals per mile of track are published as five-year averages annually since 1915 in *Proceedings,* American Railway Engineering Association. Renewals before 1915 are author's estimates based on assumptions discussed in Chapter 2.

Sources: U.S. Department of Agriculture, Forest Service, *Census of Forest Products* (Washington, D.C., 1907, 1908); *Wood Preser-*

vation Statistics; and miscellaneous data from *Proceedings,* American Wood-Preservers' Association.

Sources: U.S. Interstate Commerce Commission, *Transport Statistics in the United States,* formerly *Annual Reports of the Statistics of Railways in the United States* (Washington, D.C., annually since 1888). Summary tabulations are also taken from Association of American Railroads, Bureau of Railway Economics, *Statistics of Railroads of Class I in the United States* (Washington, D.C.), compiled annually since 1916 from reports of the ICC. "Class I" refers to line-haul railroads (formerly steam railroads) over a certain size, classified by annual revenue. They represent about 96 percent of all railroad mileage and revenues; switching and terminal companies are excluded. See also AAR, BRE, *Railroad Transportation, A Statistical Record,* 1921–1961, biennial compilation of historical series. The graphs represent official ICC accounting categories. As these vary widely with the business cycle, they are shown as three-year averages, centered on the years 1895, 1902, 1909, 1915, 1920, 1929, 1932, 1935, 1940, 1946, 1952, and 1960, to reveal long-term relative changes.

Sources: U.S. Interstate Commerce Commission, *Annual Report of the Statistics of Railways in the United States,* Section A, Abstracts of Reports Rendered by Operating Railroad Companies. Track labor refers to the track laying and surfacing account. Three-year averages are shown, in current dollars.

Sources: U.S. Department of Agriculture, *Report upon Forestry,* I (1878), and IV (1884), 119–173; Division of Forestry, *Bulletin* (No. 1, 1887); *Cross Tie Bulletin* (1920–1960); *Proceedings,* American Railway Engineering Association, Reports of the Committee on Ties (1901–1960). Figure shows ranges rather than averages, since data refer to a wide variety of conditions of production.

Source: U.S. Interstate Commerce Commission, *Annual Report of Statistics of Railways of Class I in the United States, 1937,* crossties laid in replacement, average cost in dollars of untreated tie, for each railroad company.

Sources: Class 1 railroads: U.S. Interstate Commerce Commission, *Annual Report of Statistics of Railways of Class I in the United States* were used for (1) and (2); difference (shaded) represents outlay on materials. For (3) Association of American Railroads, Bureau of Railway Economics, *Statistics on Purchasing of Materials by Class I Railways* (Washington, D.C., annually since 1923) were used. Chicago, Burlington and Quincy: (4) track labor is the sum of accounts for roadway maintenance plus track laying and surfacing, as reported in ICC *Annual Report of Statistics of Railways of Class I in the United States;* before 1900 the figure is the account for roadway repairs. Outlays for materials for track maintenance (5) are the sum of ICC accounts for rail plus ties plus ballast plus other track materials (plates and spikes). Costs of wood preserving are from annual reports of the Galesburg treating plant, MS files of the Burlington Lines, Galesburg, Illinois.

Sources: U.S. Interstate Commerce Commission, Bureau of Accounts, Cost Finding and Valuation, *Railroad Construction Guide Prices* and *Schedule of Annual Indices for Carriers by Railroad 1914 through 1960;* Association of American Railroads, Bureau of Railway Economics, *Indexes of Railroad Material Prices and Wage Rates* (Series Q–MPW–40, 1933–1960). Sources for the cost to place crosstie in track are reports of the Committee on Ties and the Committee on Track Labor, *Proceedings,* American Railway Engineering Association; for Lehigh Valley Railroad, see *Proceedings,* American Railway Engineering Association, XL (1939), and *Verbatim Record of the Temporary National Economic Com-*

mittee (Washington, D.C.: Bureau of National Affairs, Inc., 1939), hearings and Monograph No. 22, Appendix H. Source for number of employees, man-hours of all labor, number of trackmen, and number of trackmen per mile of track on Class 1 railways is U.S. Interstate Commerce Commission, *Annual Report of Statistics of Railways of Class I in the United States.* Cost to load ties on railroad cars is from annual reports of the Galesburg treating plant, MS file of the Burlington Lines, Galesburg, Illinois. The hourly wage of a section man applies to most maintenance of way employees.

Figure 25. Iron and Steel Costs in Maintenance of Way   170

Sources: For total purchases, total rail purchases, and average price and quantities of rail for all railroads, see Association of American Railroads, Bureau of Railway Economics, *Statistics on Purchasing of Materials by Class I Railways* (Washington, D.C., annually since 1923). Rail replacement is the ICC operating expense account for rail, from U.S. Interstate Commerce Commission, *Annual Report of Statistics of Railways of Class I in the United States.* The difference between the two measures of outlays on rail is due primarily to additional weight of rail, charged to Betterments rather than Operating Expenses under ICC accounting rules. Sources for average price and quantity of rail purchased by the CB&Q are steel rail files, MS, in the office of the Purchasing Agent, Burlington Lines, Chicago. Mill price of rail (f.o.b. Pittsburgh) is from John E. Partington, *Railroad Purchasing and the Business Cycle* (Washington, D.C.: Brookings Institution, 1929). Total purchases of iron and steel in hundreds of thousands of dollars include rail, tie plates, bridge steel, and so forth.

Figure 26. Railroad Purchases of Forest Products   171

Sources: For outlays of Class 1 railroads on all forest products, volume of bridge and switch ties (8) and outlay on bridge timber and car lumber, see Association of American Railroads, Bureau of Railway Economics, *Statistics on Purchasing of Materials by Class I Railways* (Washington, D.C., annually since 1923); for average price of treated (2) and untreated (3) crossties, and number of crossties renewed, see U.S. Interstate Commerce Commission, *Annual Report of Statistics of Railways of Class I in the United States*. Sources for price of southern yellow pine bridge timber in dollars per thousand board feet are U.S. Interstate Commerce Commission, Bureau of Accounts, Cost Finding and Valuation, *Railroad Construction Guide Prices* and *Schedule of Annual Indices for Carriers by Railroad 1914 through 1960*. For the Chicago, Burlington and Quincy, sources of average price of a treated crosstie (1), average price (5) and volume purchased (6) of Douglas fir bridge timber are MS accounts in the office of the Purchasing Agent, Burlington Lines, Chicago. Crosstie prices before 1909 are compiled from publications of the U.S. Department of Agriculture, *Report upon Forestry*, I, IV: *Census of Forest Products* (1907, 1908); and Division of Forestry, *Bulletin* (No. 1, 1887).

Tables

The Depletion Myth

"A Timber Famine Is Inevitable"

"Our country, we have faith to believe, is only at the beginning of its growth. Unless the vast forests of the United States can be made ready to meet the vast demands which this growth will inevitably bring, commercial disaster, that means disaster to the whole country, is inevitable. The railroads must have ties . . . The miner must have timber . . . If the present rate of forest destruction is allowed to continue, with nothing to offset it, a timber famine in the future is inevitable." [1]

That statement by President Roosevelt to the American Forest Congress in 1905 expressed one of the greatest fears of the American public. Concern, expressed as early as the 1860s and 1870s, reached its highest pitch between 1900 and 1910. The public was warned to expect the imminent depletion of the forests.

Chapter 1

The crisis never came to pass. In recent years a glut of low grades of factory lumber has been one of the greatest problems of the hardwood industry. A lack of market opportunities continues to set severe limitations on improvement of state and national forests. Acreage of land in forest uses has been increasing since about 1910. In spite of expanded uses of timber for pulp and paper, we are probably growing more cubic feet of wood annually than we were in 1910.

The difference between the expectations of 1910 and the realities of today is even sharper with respect to individual species of trees, for example, hickory. In 1911 the Forest Service and the nation's association of hickory producers investigated the "hickory problem." The annual cut was estimated at 300,000,000 feet or 3 percent of the nation's supply, which was also the entire world supply. The cut was increasing annually and was thus destroying the resource. Hickory was a wood for which "there was no satisfactory substitute, . . . so valuable for special uses that it ought not to take the place of common lumber." Uses such as crossties, posts, and bridgeplank "should not be encouraged." Forty years later, however, the Forest Service formed a "Hickory Group" among consumers to attack a hickory problem of a different sort. Because there was no demand for hickory, hickory trees were taking over the eastern hardwood forest and were occupying as much as 20 or 30 percent of timber stands. Half the hickory cut was used for ties, perhaps a million crossties a year, and the railroads were urged to use hickory on a larger scale. Annual growth of hickory, this group reported, would provide 10,000,000 ties, or 350,000,000 board feet a year, with no depletion. The market for beech in the Northeast shows the same gap between expectations of 1910 and modern realities.

Was forest depletion a myth from the first? It is true that the virgin timber of huge regions was cut, that entire commercial species were reduced to negligible quantities, and that everywhere except in the Northwest trees of very large size have been removed and are likely never to be replaced. It is true that continuation of the 1910 patterns of production and consumption of timber in the U.S. was not physically possible. Some adjustment had to be made.

But it is also true that the adjustment was not the painful one predicted by the conservationists. There were no dire consequences for consumers. There was no "commercial disaster." Nor was the adjustment the careful attention to supply that Teddy Roosevelt and Gifford Pinchot were proposing. The forests were not "made ready to meet vast demands." The solution they proposed—silviculture, the scientific growing of timber as a crop—has made modest progress, chiefly in fire protection, but it has not been a major factor in the adjustment.

What then was the nature of the adjustment? It is the thesis of this book that there were significant behavioral responses to the threat of depletion and that the most important were made by the major industrial consumers of wood, not by forest owners, managers, or lumber producers. These critical responses took the form of investments in research, specifically research in the use of wood and its substitutes.

Technological change in other sectors of the economy also helped make possible adjustments in the timber market. The effects on the forest products industries of a half century of technical improvements in transportation and business organization were dramatic, positive, and wholly unexpected. These changes did not directly affect the *physical* supply of timber substantially, but had a revolutionary impact on the *economics* of supply. In addition, their impact on agriculture was such that farmland soon began to be abandoned to forest. Indirectly the improvements in transport and management contributed to the physical supply of timber as well.

The railroads' use of timber is examined here as an example of the fundamental adjustments in the supply and demand of natural resources. It is a peculiarly valuable example for several reasons. The railroads were large consumers, of vital importance in the timber market. Their outlays on timber were and still are large enough to influence their total operations. The railroad industry is old enough to allow us to trace its use of timber through the full term of evolution of forestry consciousness in America, down to the present. Finally, the railroads' importance in the economy as a whole has made them an industry whose accounts, business organization, and technology can be documented more fully than most.

The railroad crosstie plays a large part in this story, and its history was not undertaken as an exercise in documenting the trivial. (Some might consider a hundred-million-dollar a year industry such as treated crossties as trivial.) It is rather to be seen as an example of business decision making and public policy making in the natural resource area. It illustrates the interplay of private enterprise, government agencies, scientific research, and public opinion.

In the early 1900s the railroads consumed about one-fifth of the nation's timber harvest. The largest single use was for crossties, but they also used large amounts of bridge timber and piling and a variety of other timber products, in car construction and repair, maintenance of telegraph lines, snow fences, tunnels, wharves, buildings, and platforms. Labor, fuel, iron, and timber have always been the largest items of the railroads' annual expenditure, and except fuel they are the major items of railroad capital. While the railroads have been recognized as large consumers of iron and steel, with important influence on the development of steel and its manufacturing technology, they have had an equally important influence on the forest products industries.

If a timber famine should occur, surely the railroads would

feel the pinch. In the early 1900s the railroads were advised to expect to replace their wood bridges, crossties, buildings, and rolling stock with metal or concrete. Railroad consumption of timber did indeed decline dramatically both in absolute and relative terms. It fell from 20 to 25 percent of the timber cut in 1909 to 3 or 4 percent in the 1960s (exclusive of pulpwood). Yet, the volume of timber purchased for railroading is still large, on the order of one billion board feet per year. Large wood trestles are nearly as common as they were fifty years ago. Wood ties are still used routinely on most American railroads. The railroads obtain all the crossties they want, at an annual cost of $100,000,000 (including treatment, but excluding track labor), as compared with $60,000,000 or $75,000,000 in 1908. If these figures in current dollars are reduced to real values, there has certainly been no increase in the annual outlays for crossties. Today's crossties are larger on the average and are more uniform in quality. We must infer that the railroads have not suffered substantial ill effects from timber shortage.

The behavior of the railroad as a consumer is especially interesting because it is the best-known "big business" that can be studied throughout a period of growth and a period of relative stagnation. How did the railroads respond to forecasts of wood shortages? How did they make their decisions about research? What were the payoffs? How did their research affect their demand for timber? What effects did they have on supply? How did they modify their own expectations?

Railroad uses of timber are diverse and complex enough to represent timber use of other large industrial consumers. The changes in railroad uses parallel closely the evolution of timber utilization in mining, communications, and construction industries. The case of the railroad consumers might well be supplemented by studies of wood pulp and chemical industries. In general the case of the railroad gives a fair picture of the experience of other users of round timber, construction lumber, and manufacturing lumber.

Today few Americans feel threatened by timber famine. The forester and woodlot owner find no sale for their timber blown down in a hurricane. The city dweller who goes back to Maine, Massachusetts, or Georgia finds the forests have blotted out the rural scene he remembers from childhood. The average American is more concerned with new issues of conservation—the crisis of water, depletion of oil wells, pollution of the air, levels of radioactivity and toxic chemicals, and exhaustion of the soil. Does the national experience of forest values provide any perspective on these current concerns? In the timber story, it looks as if somehow we succeeded in avoiding the "inevitable." Yet we did not do it by following the doctor's advice. We need to examine whether our public fears and concerns were helpful in finding an adjustment. Can we predict more accurately the impact of technology? Can we prescribe more sensibly?

A major question in all conservation issues is the role of public resource management agencies. In what ways do these agencies influence market expectations and the economic behavior of private industries? The expectations and effectiveness of public agencies are affected by their organizational structure, their purposes and responsibilities. How effectively has the Forest Service, for instance, "conserved" timber? Why did the Forest Service fail to foresee and press the eventual adjustment? Why was its own proposal—"Grow More Wood!"—not the one adopted? What credit or discredit should be given to its molder and hero, Gifford Pinchot? Relations between public foresters and railroad men provide new insights into the more general problem of relating goals of public policy and goals of private industry in the management of resources.

The story is told roughly in chronological sequence. Railroad uses of timber reached their peak in the 1880s (Chapter 2). Public anxiety about the cutting of the forests and the hope that planting was the panacea were voiced at that time (Chapter 3). By the 1890s the railroads were developing new research methods and new technologies that could cut their use of timber, but they did not put these techniques into practice (Chapter 4). There was a crisis in the early 1900s when railroad men and conservationists joined hands (Chapter 5). But by 1915 there were substantial differences of theory, expectation, and policy between the two groups, and the railroads began to apply their new know-how (Chapter 6). After World War I technical progress was rapid and began to pay off (Chapter 7). Public resource agencies showed strong interest. During the depression, however, foresters and public agencies gradually returned "for the duration" to their old themes of depletion and the silvicultural remedy, at variance with railroad practice and the experience of a generation (Chapter 8). In the concluding chapter examples from the entire century of railroad and forest history are drawn together to show how adjustments of supply and demand occur in the natural resource area, with emphasis on the industrial consumer's role.

The history of railway uses of timber is a case study of long-term changes in the pattern of use of one major resource. It differs critically from the classic fairy tale of American history and the traditional foresters' version of forest history. This analysis of relations between two major sectors of the economy —railroads and timber—brings into new prominence the role of the consumer and the role of product research in the management of natural resources. It demonstrates that the industrial consumer has substantial power to bring about greater efficiency in the use of resources and to confound predictions that look only at his past habits and fail to take into account his powers of choice and change.

"The Insatiable Juggernaut of the Vegetable World"

The railroad, known in most languages as "the iron road," might as easily be called "the wooden road." American railroads in particular promptly became large consumers of timber. The prairie lines built in the 1870s and 1880s were constructed almost entirely of wood except for the rails, spikes, car wheels, and locomotives. The track structure alone contained a large volume of wood in the 2,640 (more or less) crossties per mile. Substantial new mileage was being added until World War I, and, what was more serious, the entire volume of wood crossties rotted out and had to be replaced every six or seven years on the average. The railroads were consuming approximately one-fifth to one-fourth of the nation's timber cut and were paying more for forest products than for rail. Their pattern of consumptive use of wood, or rapid replacement, was typical of most uses of timber in the American economy before World War I.

Satisfying the immense appetite of the railroads for timber was, clearly, big business. The markets were initially local and diverse in their technical and business organization, but as the railroads grew into a national network, the crosstie and bridge timber markets also became integrated into a complex system with a definite geographical pattern of prices and technical practices.

Prices are a vital clue in the interpretation of economic factors affecting supply. During the thirty years after the Civil War, when the growth of the railway timber supply industry was most dramatic, what happened to prices? I have analyzed the records of the Burlington Lines to obtain evidence concerning prices.

The Wooden Road

The first railroads in England and the United States experimented with wood, stone, and cast iron ties laid with wood or iron rails. Most of the earliest American steam railroads were designed for stone ties and wood rails faced with strap iron. Stone ties, it was thought, would bear the heavy loads of steam engines. The cost of hauling materials to the railroad site in the relatively undeveloped American countryside was, however, so great that engineers substituted wood for stone ties where stone could not be quarried within a few miles of the railroad. In addition, stone ties broke, and engineers began to argue that the elasticity of timber made it more satisfactory for ties. Though these primitive roads were sometimes ballasted, tamping was poor, and the bearing surface was uneven. The uneven transmission of the load caused ties to break. Thus, the wood crosstie quickly became a key element in railway construction and maintenance.

By 1850 the United States had nine thousand miles of railroads. The structure was generally iron rail with iron spikes, although some lines, such as the first few miles of the Burlington, had wood rails faced with iron strap. Wood was used for all other members, the ties, joints, guardrails, bridges, and fencing. The fuel was wood. The cars were entirely of wood, and even in tenders and engines the load-bearing members and brake beams were wood.

By the time of the Civil War the eastern railways had switched to coal for fuel, although they continued to use considerable kindling, preferably hardwood. Buildings were still heated with wood. Wood trestles were common in the South, and wood trusses could still be found in the North, but covered wood bridges were regarded as anachronisms, vulnerable to fire and expensive to maintain. Stone and earth embankments were considered safe and economical. The first steel railroad bridges were built in the 1870s. Masonry was preferred for industrial buildings. The largest demand for wood was for tie renewals at the rate of about four hundred per mile of track per year, or 15 percent of total mileage.

At the same time transcontinental links were being built with the help of railroad land grants. The railroads across the prairies had a new appetite for timber. Like prairie farmers, the grassland rail lines faced novel problems. As a developmental venture in a sparsely populated area, the prairie railway had to be lightly and swiftly built so that it would quickly begin to yield some return on the investment. It could be rebuilt gradually, more substantially, when traffic, capital, and labor were in greater supply. Under these conditions wood was an attractive material. Low in initial cost, of light weight to ship or float, wood could be handled by unskilled labor and framed or fabricated to standard sizes with simple equipment at the building site. Wood could be patched, replaced, and rebuilt more easily than the "permanent" materials. The prairie railroads such as the Burlington, Central Pacific, Union Pacific, and Santa Fe began to use wood in great volume for bridging and tunneling, snow fences, culverts, and telegraph poles.[1] The methods of bridge construction on the prairie railroads were essentially those devised by Hermann Haupt for military use during the Civil War. Round timber was used to save sawing, and all-wood pile trestles were preferred where the elevation was not too great.

The same evolution was typical of many American patterns of timber use. The settlers brought European ideas of the desirability of stone masonry, brick, and earthwork or metals for permanent structures—homes, factories, churches, public buildings—but the facts of economic supply, the high cost of transport and labor, and the urgency of demand all favored the use of wood rather than other materials. These pressures, and therefore the consumption of wood, increased as settlement reached the prairies.

In the 1870s the prairie railroads began to discover the high costs of repairs, renewals, replacements, and improvements in their lightly built systems. Traffic had increased. The country's railroad mileage was still expanding rapidly. These three facts—new ways of using wood on prairie lines, new high rates of replacement, and a high rate of new construction—added up to enormous purchases of wood by the railroads.

From the 1870s to 1900 the railroads consumed one-fifth to one-fourth of the nation's annual timber production. The use of wood per mile probably reached a maximum about 1880, and increasing mileage accounts for great total consumption in the 1880s and 1890s. These trends in railroads' use of wood paralleled those of the construction industry, domestic fuel, mine props, and farm uses. These uses, too, probably peaked in their dependence on timber as the basic material in the late 1870s, but rapid industrial growth increased the total demand for wood further in the 1880s and 1890s. The use of wood as an industrial fuel was, however, already declining rapidly.

The rapid rate of replacement was a matter of the length of service that could be obtained from a particular species of timber in a particular type of use. Crossties had a shorter life than the same timbers in most other uses because of their exposure to moisture. The average service life expected of the best white oak crossties in various parts of the country is shown on the map (fig. 1). Less durable species of timber had been used in the prairies, the central South, and far northern states—areas outside the region of large white oak stands.

The growing demand for ties is estimated in the following table, based on average track construction with 2,640 ties per mile. Annual renewals are conservatively estimated at 350 per mile, and the average cut of ties at 200 per forested acre.

Table 1. Crosstie estimates, 1870–1910.

	Miles of track	Millions of ties renewed each year	Millions of ties used in new construction	Total millions of ties each year	Thousands of acres of timber
1870	60,000	21	18	39	195
1880	107,000	37	21	58	290
1890	200,000	70	19	89	445
1900	259,000	91			
1910	357,000	124		124[a]	620[a]

[a] "Consumption of Wood Preservatives and Quantity of Wood Treated in the United States in 1910," U.S. Department of Agriculture, Forest Service, *Circular* (No. 186, 1911).

It would be necessary to allot an equal quantity of timber for original bridge and construction lumber, although buildings—painted and roofed—did not deteriorate rapidly or have to be replaced so soon. By 1890 the railroads were using well over

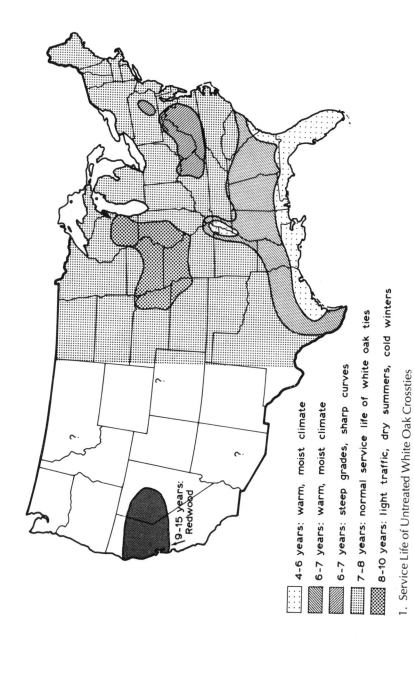

4-6 years: warm, moist climate

6-7 years: warm, moist climate

6-7 years: steep grades, sharp curves

7-8 years: normal service life of white oak ties

8-10 years: light traffic, dry summers, cold winters

9-15 years: Redwood

1. Service Life of Untreated White Oak Crossties

three billion board feet of timber annually, or half a million acres of forest for permanent way and buildings (car lumber excluded). The railroad was indeed an "insatiable Juggernaut of the vegetable world." [2]

Sources of Supply

Maps of tie markets and prices about 1880 (figs. 2 and 3) reveal the central facts of supply and demand. Demand was greatest in the prairies where railroad construction was occurring. Supply was governed by the natural stands of preferred species (see figs. 4 to 7) and the available transportation. Ties rarely were hauled more than five miles by wagon, but the 1870s and 1880s were the heyday of long hauls by water and rail. There was great variation in price from place to place. The nationwide range for a single group of species, the white oaks, was wide, from ten to eighty cents; this was due to the high cost of transport and to variation in sizes of ties and local wages. In the short run, tie prices were said to be linked to the price of mule feed.

In contrast to iron and steel rail expenditures, railroad outlays for ties were spread widely and made an important contribution to farm capital and purchasing power in the least developed regions of the country. Expenditures for ties were largely for labor and hauling. For example, about 1880 one major railroad paid thirty cents for hewing and hauling ties to the right-of-way, a cent for contractor's working capital, and an additional seven and a half cents for inspection, loading, stores, and distribution to points of use. The cost of labor for inserting ties in the track was roughly ten cents more. The total cost in place was then forty-eight and a half cents, or an annual cost over an eight-year life of about six cents.

On the map of hardwood tie markets in 1882 (fig. 2) the fifty-cent price contour delineates metropolitan zones of high

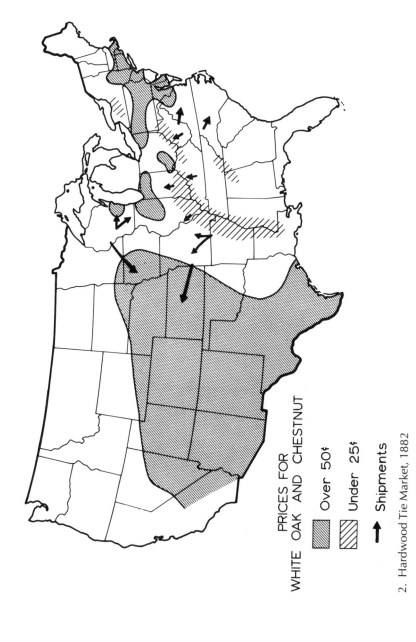

PRICES FOR
WHITE OAK AND CHESTNUT

Over 50¢

Under 25¢

Shipments

2. Hardwood Tie Market, 1882

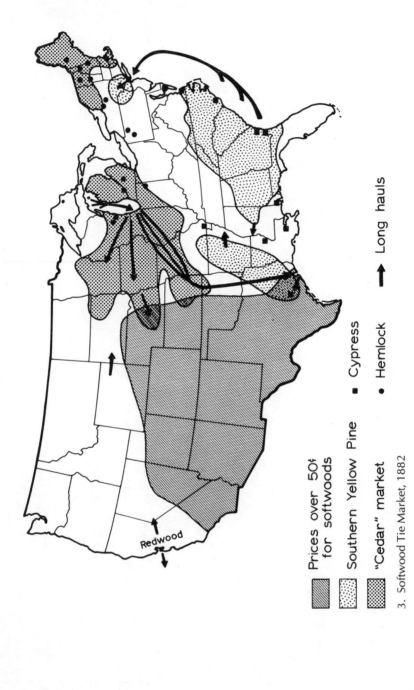

Prices over 50¢ for softwoods

Southern Yellow Pine

"Cedar" market

Cypress

Hemlock

Long hauls

Redwood

3. Softwood Tie Market, 1882

prices—between fifty and eighty cents for white oak or chestnut ties. In these regions the urban populations pushed prices of wood up by their demand for firewood, building lumber, and industrial charcoal and by the high value of land in agricultural uses. The railways in this region were among the oldest in the country. They had exhausted their local supplies and made it worthwhile to remove timber for construction lumber. A southwestern zone of prices over fifty cents reflects the scarcity of natural stands of timber and the low density of the rail network and labor. Large shipments out of the Rockies did not reduce prices because of additional transport costs.

A zone of low prices, twenty-five cents or less, appears along the Ohio and Mississippi valleys. Crossties were moved in barges towed (pushed) by steamboats on the Mississippi and Ohio rivers and major tributaries, the Green, Cumberland, Kentucky, and Tennessee rivers. This was the backbone of the white oak tie supply, and prices rose with distance from the axis. The range of natural growth of other species is shown in figures 4–7, but tends to exaggerate supply, as stands are not substantial on the fringes.

The map of prices in softwood tie markets (fig. 3) also reflects the dominant role of the white oak supply zone. Oak ties probably accounted for about two-thirds of all ties produced before 1890. Softwood ties were substituted on the fringes of that zone. Cypress, a superior species because of its natural durability, was used on the lines that tapped its natural stands. Southern yellow pine was employed locally and shipped by sea to New York City, a zone of high demand. In the north hemlock was used where it was locally available, and white cedar was shipped through Chicago to the zone of high demand and new construction in the plains as far south as Texas and Mexico. On the West Coast the soft but decay-resistant redwood was preferred. Except redwood, which was split with the ax, all the timbers were hewed.

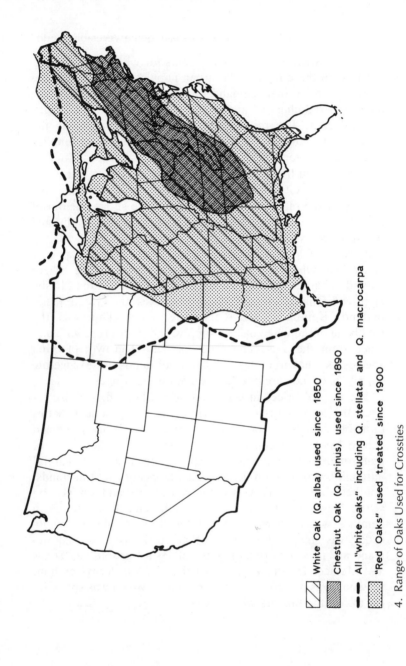

White Oak (Q. alba) used since 1850

Chestnut Oak (Q. prinus) used since 1890

All "white oaks" including Q. stellata and Q. macrocarpa

"Red Oaks" used treated since 1900

4. Range of Oaks Used for Crossties

18

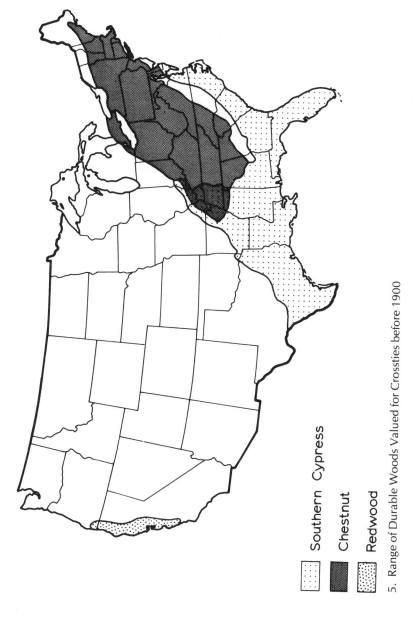

Southern Cypress

Chestnut

Redwood

5. Range of Durable Woods Valued for Crossties before 1900

19

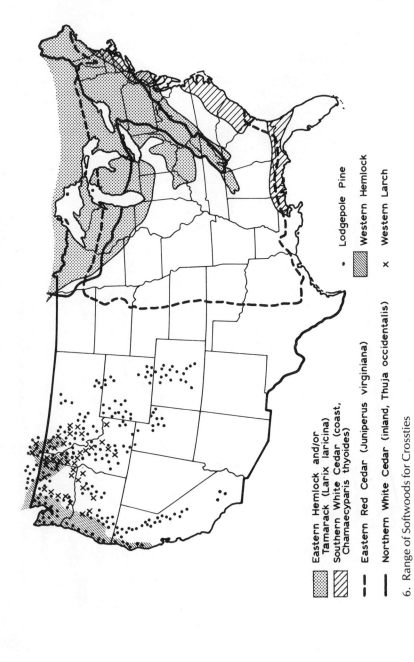

Eastern Hemlock and/or
Tamarack (Larix laricina)
Southern White Cedar (coast,
Chamaecyparis thyoides)

--- Eastern Red Cedar (Juniperus virginiana)

—— Northern White Cedar (inland, Thuja occidentalis)

• Lodgepole Pine

▨ Western Hemlock

× Western Larch

6. Range of Softwoods for Crossties

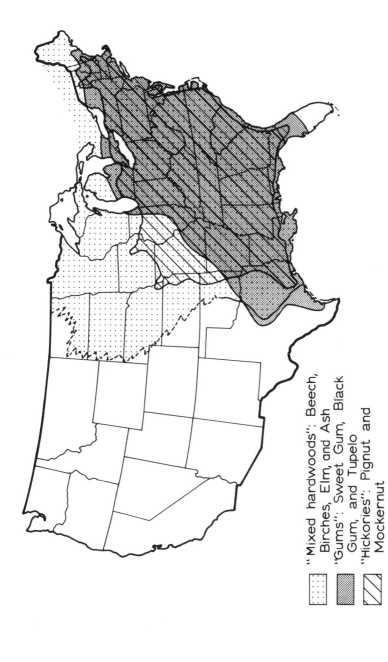

"Mixed hardwoods": Beech, Birches, Elm, and Ash
"Gums": Sweet Gum, Black Gum, and Tupelo
"Hickories": Pignut and Mockernut

7. Range of Hardwoods Substituted When Seasoned and Treated

Most tie makers preferred young "second-growth" timber. Each tree was hewed into a single tie. The size varied, usually eight feet long, with a five- to eight-inch face, six or seven inches thick. Railroads generally required that ties be cut in winter. They preferred heartwood to sapwood. (Sapwood meant the younger outer rings of lighter colored wood in which sap was found.) These restrictions were based on the belief that spring sap hastened decay in the ties. About 1900 the theory was proved false and irrelevant, but the restrictions were sound, nonetheless, because spring and summer weather conditions of moisture and warmth were favorable to the growth of fungi, the agents of decay. Winter-cut ties stood several months under weather conditions less favorable to decay. By the time they were laid in track in the spring, they were half-seasoned or sufficiently dry to resist fungi. Summer-cut ties decayed in the woods or along the right-of-way, because no precautions were taken to season, aerate, or disinfect the ties or to hurry shipment. A few railroads specified how ties were to be piled on the right-of-way, but there was no standard practice. The New Orleans and Northeastern actually ordered tie makers to scatter the ties on the ground for easy inspection; this practice subjected ties to moisture and contamination of fungus spores.

Each of the regional tie markets had its own peculiarities. In the oak market, other hardwoods were accepted up to 10 or 20 percent of the lot. Black locust especially was appreciated because it resisted decay. Chestnut was widely substituted in New England and the Middle Atlantic states. Railroads purchased ties in small lots from farmers along their lines. A single railroad was the only market for most of these farmers. The farmer needed extra work in winter, and the railroad hired him at a low wage. Railroads often refused to haul ties as freight in order to restrict the local market to their own control.[3]

In regions of early settlement and large demand for wood the railroads began to haul wood long distances by water in the 1870s. Coastal shipping provided cypress, cedar, and longleaf pine from the South. Cypress and cedar had long been preferred where they were available locally because they resisted decay. Longleaf pine was a dense wood, and rolling stock was still light enough so that this grade of pine withstood the punishment about as well as oak. Southern yellow pine (longleaf) was shipped even farther for bridge timber than for crossties. Because it was impossible to distinguish the several species of pine—longleaf, shortleaf, and loblolly—by inspection of the wood, fraud was common in this market. The railroads believed longleaf was superior to the others in hardness and resistance to decay. Producers falsified origin of timber, and inspectors did not know how to judge quality independent of the source.

Adjacent to the prairies, tie making became big business. In Indiana and Illinois ties were cash crop and local currency. In Missouri ties had been produced to meet the demands of railroads as they were built out of St. Louis, but about 1880 the market expanded enormously. Oak ties from the Ozarks and the lowlands were exported into the prairies, the South, and the Midwest. At that time tie contractors appeared; they provided working capital to keep tie hackers (hewers of ties) in business and operated as middlemen between railroad agents and producers. The contractors were responsible for the gradual development of this area as a major tie-producing region. St. Louis became the chief tie market of the nation after World War I.

Ties cut on the western frontier were also shipped into the prairie zone of demand. Tie manufacture was often on a grand scale in the Rockies, and tie hacking was one of the most rugged and most lucrative jobs of the mountain frontier. The ties were hewed to size in the woods, hauled out by mule, driven on the spring flood, then rafted to points on the railroads.

The demand for large commercial imports of ties into the prairies created opportunities for wheeling and dealing, theft and fraud in the lower Ohio Valley and the Rockies. The Illinois Central Railroad, for example, found itself purchasing ties that had been illegally cut on its own lands.[4] A federal law of 1878 that gave railroads the right to take timber and stone from adjacent land for construction purposes was abused on a grand scale. The land entry laws were also abused for timber stripping. Ties cut on unsurveyed federal land in the Rockies were sold to the Union Pacific and Canadian Pacific. In 1879 the Department of the Interior sent agents to examine the depredations. These special agents of the General Land Office reported stolen during the decade 1886–1896 $7,000,000 worth of stumpage or 10,000,000 board feet of timber. Most of the stolen timber was probably made into ties, a total of about 300,000 ties, which was a very modest contribution to the tie market over ten years. Suits were brought for market values of $24,000,000, but the amounts recovered were of the order of $1,000,000.[5]

From the northern frontier as well, ties were brought to the deficit region of the prairies. Cedar, tamarack, and hemlock ties and cedar poles and fence posts began to move in the 1870s from the north by lake schooner and lake steamer to Chicago and then by rail to the prairies. As its rail connections grew, the Chicago tie market also grew—at a phenomenal rate between 1880 and 1892. On this frontier, as in St. Louis and in the Rockies, unprecedented demand generated new forms of enterprise suited to larger scales of operation. Individual deals were made for millions of ties at once by operators such as Edward Ayer, who controlled two-fifths of the Chicago cedar tie market. Like other big businessmen at the time, Ayer entered pooling agreements with his competitors to supply the docks at Chicago, then made his money on shipping deals involving large volumes. His shipments to the Mexican Central Railway represented about a million ties a year, thousands of carloads of freight. He shipped via the Santa Fe, Burlington, Wabash, and other railroads in the "Omaha pool" to Kansas City, then via the Santa Fe to Mexico. For years he paid the Santa Fe $700 to $900 a day on freight. In turn, the Santa Fe purchased millions of ties for its own construction projects. The Burlington began to buy hundreds of thousands of cedar ties from Ayer in 1880, in order to obtain a "fair share" of his shipments to Mexico. In 1886 Ayer made one deal to sell 1,000,000 ties to the Burlington and another with the Santa Fe for 2,600,000 ties, 40,000 poles, and 2,000,000 posts.

Larger Purchases—At What Price?

In spite of the wide geographical variation of crosstie prices, prices at a given point of use show no upward trend over the twelve years 1880–1892.[6] The Burlington's purchasing records provide additional evidence and some clues to the reasons for stable prices. The map (fig. 8) shows the timing of construction of various segments of the Burlington system, consolidated in the late 1870s. Crosstie prices and rates of replacement on the Burlington appear stable in the 1880s and 1890s (fig. 9). There is no evidence for any rise in the cost of engine kindling. Prices of bridge timber behaved much like those of the wrought iron and cast iron hardware used for bridges, that is, up and down with the business cycle. In contrast, the price of steel rail fell steadily for thirty years after the Civil War, thanks to innovations in manufacture and economies of scale as the market grew. But because railroads adopted ever heavier rail to carry heavier loads, their total outlay on rail did not fall until the 1890s, and they directed most of their research in the 1870s and 1880s toward obtaining longer service life from iron and steel rail.

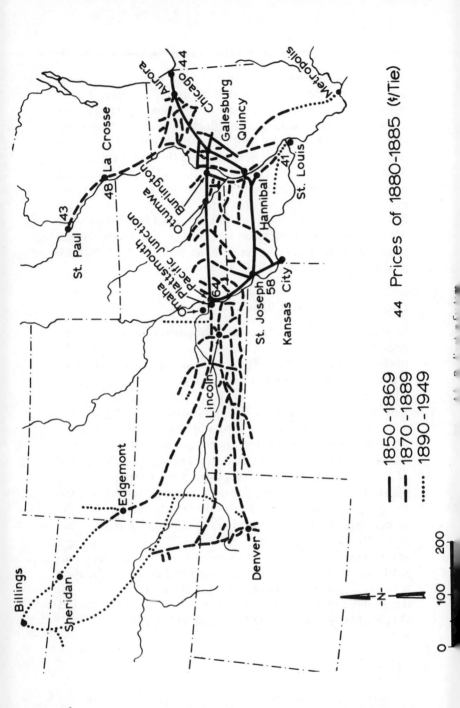

44 Prices of 1880-1885 (¢/Tie)

1850-1869
1870-1889
1890-1949

Billings
Sheridan
Edgemont
Denver
Lincoln
Omaha
Plattsmouth
Pacific Junction
Burlington
Ottumwa
St. Paul
La Crosse
Aurora
Chicago
Galesburg
Quincy
Hannibal
St. Louis
Metropolis
St. Joseph
Kansas City

43
48
44
41
64
58

0   100   200

—N—

26

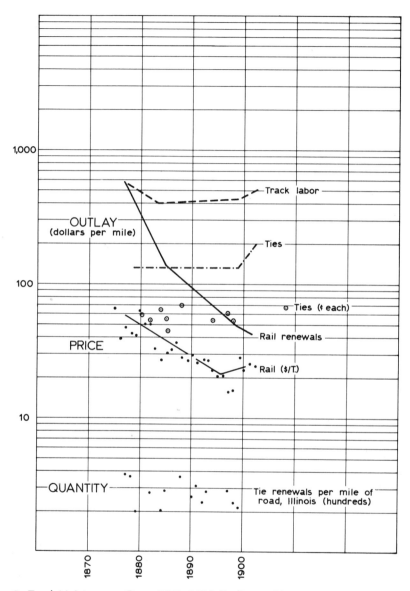

9. Track Maintenance Costs, 1870–1902, Burlington Lines

Although the Warren and Pearson wholesale price index declines nearly 20 percent over the 1880s, I have not deflated prices, for several reasons. Any such index is strongly affected by the components (timber, iron and steel, labor) whose price behavior relative to each other we want to examine. The available indices are derived from New York or other local markets uniquely affected by changes in the geographical transport cost structure. I would argue that the framework for managerial attention (an investment in time) to crossties lies in the production function and market price experience of the railroad firm, not in a general equilibrium framework. To the Burlington, and to most other railroad managements, timber prices *appeared* to be stable, as expressed in current dollars, and their total outlays on timber were stable relative to total outlays for rail and labor, the other major inputs to maintenance of way. These, I contend, are the relevant determinants of whether management recognizes a problem of increasing relative scarcity which calls for new economizing behavior. In the 1870s and 1880s, therefore, timber prices cause no special concern to management, and no special effort to reduce timber use. In view of the rapidly rising consumption owing to increased mileage of the Burlington and competing lines, how was this possible?

In the 1860s the Burlington was importing large structural bridge timbers from the Great Lakes region. The finest white pine was used for bridges and buildings, while high-grade white oak was used for piles and ties. About 1880 Georgia yellow pine was imported from much greater distances for those uses of highest value. The pattern of supplying low-value uses, such as crossties, also changed. Gradually in the 1870s the Burlington extended the zone from which it drew crossties. Softwoods came through Chicago from the Great Lakes states and Canada. Oak ties were brought from the Ozarks over the Chicago and Alton Railroad to Kansas, and oak was supplied from Wisconsin to build the Chicago, Burlington and Northern line to St. Paul. The very lowest grade of wood, engine kindling, continued to be supplied locally.

The long-distance imports seem to have been substituted at no increase in price. Old sources were cut out, and often the forest land was brought under cultivation, but improved access to new regions apparently made it possible to obtain timber of the same quality at the same price. Changes in the unit cost of transport compensated for greater distances of timber haul, so that more ties could be supplied at the old price.

Improved access was the result of many events. Local access improved as settlement proceeded, local roads were built, and farm labor and teams became available for hauling. The cost of hauling kindling by wagon to the railroad was about 35 percent of its total cost to the railroad. Construction of feeder lines and elaboration of the consumer railroad's own system made it possible to tap new local supplies of kindling and ties. Lines were extended to the foothills of the Rockies, and ties were brought out by stream drive. The construction of rail lines in the hinterland of southern ports also made it possible for large quantities of timber to reach cheap water transport and enter the larger market. The integration of the long-distance rail network made it possible to ship timber long distances overland. Regional price differentials remained, as shown on the map of the Burlington system (fig. 8), but long hauls were common and cheap.

In the 1870s and 1880s the railroads created an enormous demand for timber, but at the same time they created the means of supplying that demand without change of price. From the consumers' point of view, then, no general depletion or scarcity was perceptible. There was, consequently, no incentive for them to reduce their consumption. The juggernaut grew and prospered, more voracious than ever.

"How Simple It Would Be"

Public concern about destruction of the forests gradually became a powerful emotional issue, and it was political dynamite. The nation's large consumers of timber were not generally suffering, as Chapter 2 shows, but their concern was nevertheless rooted in certain kinds of experience. We can identify four distinct strands of experience, although we cannot be certain about their relative importance. Out of the total experience, Americans generated an interpretation and an idealized solution. The railroads took a significant part in developing the theory and the panacea. Both would affect public thinking for a century.

One strand in the experience was, of course, the swiftness, drama, and ruthlessness of the cutting of the American forest. By the 1850s the trans-Appalachian forests were being cut rapidly to develop new land for agriculture, and it appeared that the forests were being destroyed forever, not merely harvested. American attitudes toward forest destruction had always been ambiguous. Perry Miller has sketched the appearance in the 1830s and 1840s of a Romantic nostalgia for the wilderness.[1] Wilderness symbolized integrity, purity, judgment, and salvation contrasted with the defilement of town and "civilization." Miller asserts that this was the mark of a national identity expressed in the literary works of James Fenimore Cooper, Herman Melville, Henry David Thoreau, and Walt Whitman and the paintings of the Hudson River school, for example, Thomas Cole's 1848 series, *The Lament of the Forest*.

Even where land was not intended for permanent clearing, the timber was harvested by clear cutting, which did not favor quick regeneration of the forest. Clear cutting was often followed by forest fires. As Chapter 2 demonstrated, timber consumption was increasing rapidly in the 1870s and 1880s and was reaching into all forested regions. At that time influential businessmen and prominent families were beginning to do much traveling and sight-seeing by rail, and the sight of logged off land and burned forests made a strong impression. Both are devastating sights, inflammatory to the imagination. The psychological aspects of forestry should not be overstated, but the attitude documented by Miller for the early nineteenth century and apparent in forestry journals for the second half of the century[2] reveals an intensely personal, emotionally charged experience that is peculiar to the American forestry movement.

A second element in the American attitude toward destruction of forests was the British and European experience. The great "conservationist" writer of the seventeenth century, John Evelyn,[3] was read in this country. Royal protection of forests, domestic and colonial, was a strict and long-established practice that ensured the survival of wooden navies as well as upper-class hunting privileges. In eighteenth- and nineteenth-century Britain, nevertheless, charcoal for expanded metallurgical and chemical industries produced local depletion and substantial price increases for timber in urban areas. The industrial revolution can be interpreted in part as a process of substitution of mineral fuels and materials for wood.[4] By the mid-nineteenth century thoughtful American travelers and readers knew that Britain and the German states consumed much less timber, had strict laws regulating forests, paid much higher prices for timber and timbered land, and made substantial investments in planting, protecting, harvesting, and handling timber. It was not unreasonable for them to project the current European conditions as the American future. The gap seemed so wide that they conceived of the transition as a dreadful crisis or burden.

Among the organizers of American forestry were John A. Warder, who reported on German forestry on his return from the World's Fair at Vienna (1873), and George Perkins Marsh, the much-traveled geographer, linguist, and diplomat who stirred the American Association for the Advancement of Science in 1873 to appoint a committee to study American forests.[5] This led promptly and directly to creation of a federal office of Forester. Since the Americans had no experience of planting or management of forests, they were inevitably influenced by theories and practices forged in the economic conditions of Europe.

Consumer experience of "depletion" was a third factor. As early as the Civil War there were pockets of local depletion. In eastern metropolitan areas wood was expensive. Railroads, still small and local, perceived or anticipated a crisis when the white oak species of timber within five miles of their own line was cut out. Bringing off-line timber meant added out-of-pocket costs for transport and a threatening dependence on outsiders. As we saw in Chapter 2, the problem was largely solved in the 1870s and 1880s, as railroads were consolidated into larger systems and the network of long-distance lines was completed. By the 1880s most consumers were not suffering and were being supplied with greater and greater quantities of timber at no increase in unit price. The memory of local shortages contributed, nevertheless, to the general alarm and to the railroad managers' awareness of what any "general depletion" would mean to them.

The early experiences of local depletion led to the first complete exposition of a theory of railroad forestry in 1866, by Andrew Fuller. It appears to be one of the first homegrown American conceptions of commercial forestry. Fuller predicted general depletion and proposed planting trees all along railroad rights-of-way. According to his plans, trees planted four feet apart, eleven thousand to the acre, would be thinned for hoop poles after five to eight years. Every three to four years after that, ten-foot trees of tie size with a ten-cent stumpage value, could be harvested. Sprouts would then produce a perpetual crop, and each acre's harvest at three- or four-year intervals would be worth two hundred to three hundred dollars. "Even where railroads have penetrated regions abundantly supplied, we soon find that all along its track timber soon becomes scarce. For every railroad in the country requires a continued forest from one end to the other of its lines to supply it with ties, fuel, and lumber for building their cars. Cars are continually wearing out, ties are rotting, and the time is not far distant when these great monopolies will find that it would have been cheaper for them to have grown their own timber than to have depended on others to supply them. How simple it would be to have a few acres of forest trees every few miles all along and contiguous to the line."[6]

Implicit in Fuller's plan were certain crucial assumptions —fallacies—that persisted in American forestry theories for the next half century and have only gradually been laid to rest. Foresters today would be astonished at his expectations of growth rates for hardwoods. Geographers might well question his choice of prime value land for forestry use. The businessman would notice immediately his failure to count his interest costs, and railroad men would remark the absence of alternative solutions such as reducing consumption. Fuller's arboriculture was excusable, indeed constructive, in the 1860s, when practically nothing was known in America about growth rates or wood preservation, but his simple solution became popular among railroad men and the general public to the point where it was almost indestructible.

By the 1870s the prairie experience became a fourth major strand in concern for forests. Romantic nostalgia for the wilderness, European contrasts, and erroneous expectations of regional depletion in the East prepared a forest consciousness, but I would argue that the experience of natural scarcity of timber in the prairies was more important to thinking on American forestry than man-made changes in the once forested regions. Perception of change was sharpened by the prairie experience; "depletion" of eastern timber, for example, became alarming when settlers contemplated the special problems of the western timberless region. Their concern was magnified by a willingness to identify all the problems of the Plains with this distinctive lack of forests. Drought, for example, they interpreted as a result of the absence of forests.[7] European austerity in the use of wood looked threatening to the plains dweller who depended on it as his chief fuel and construction material.

This view of the importance of the prairie experience is suggested, first, by the personalities involved in forestry organizations and, second, by their initial and persistent emphasis on planting trees in the treeless regions. Arbor Day was first observed in Nebraska in 1872. The American Forestry Association, founded in 1875, included botanists, landscape gardeners, horticulturists, and estate owners, with a large proportion of its supporters from the Midwest. Academics, practitioners, and local amateurs and fanatics were thoroughly mixed. The composition of the group indicates a concern with arboriculture or tree planting and aesthetics, not the management of natural forests nor any clear commercial objective. Many members were interested in promoting individual American species. They focused on the fast-growing and hardy species that could be planted in the prairies. Warder had identified the *Catalpa speciosa,* and Marsh had publicized the environmental tolerance of the black locust. E. E. Barney, a railroad car company manager in Dayton, Ohio, published a pamphlet testifying to the value of the catalpa. Representatives of the northern prairies emphasized the value of the cottonwood and willows. In southern California Ellwood Cooper promoted the Australian gums (eucalyptus). None of these had or has today commercial timber value in this country, but all are fast growing, hardy, and identified with American regionalism.

In the 1880s the arboriculturists waxed more and more optimistic about the commercial opportunities of prairie planting and the special case of the railroads. Annual forest congresses were dominated by men from Ohio, Indiana, and the prairie states of the United States and Canada. At all the meetings there were papers on railroad forestry, prairie planting, and railroad fires. Hough and Warder gave papers on tree planting by railroad companies. At the Cincinnati congress, in 1883, there were speeches on catalpa and locust trees. In the forestry journals, such as Charles Sprague Sargent's *Garden and Forest,* many articles appeared on railroad forestry, planting, and the potential of the catalpa and black locust. A paper at the St. Paul congress, also in 1883, was typical of the extreme arboriculturists. The author expected it would cost five thousand dollars to purchase, fence, plant, and cultivate forty acres of "good western land." With catalpa, white ash, Russian mulberry, or black walnut, he believed that in sixteen to twenty years the trees would produce a forty-thousand-dollar crop of ties and posts. "The motive power in this the 19th century is money—the love of money or the anticipation of money! Then let us consider tree-planting in its true light . . . the light of money-making . . . we strike the keynote, whose music will vibrate throughout the length and breadth of our western plains. Our capitalists, east, west, north, or south, all invest their money for the purpose of increase; their sole objective is to accumulate . . . Forest tree planting will make a safer investment and bring in larger and more satisfactory returns than any other business that a man can embark in." [8]

State timber culture acts and a federal timber culture act were passed in the 1870s, making prairie land available to those who would plant trees. For example, 160 acres were patented to the person who would plant 10 acres to timber and keep it healthy for eight years. The acts were ineffectual or worse and encouraged settlers to plant commercially worthless species solely to gain entry.

During the 1870s and early 1880s railroads took part in planting the prairies just as they took part in promoting their settlement. The Burlington and Missouri River Railroad, later part of the Burlington Lines, invested fourteen thousand dollars in plantations between 1872 and 1874. Willow, cottonwood, and other local timbers were set out in Kansas and Nebraska under contract with Robert Douglas' nursery. They were not regarded as tie- or lumber-producing ventures, but were conceived as snow fences, windbreaks, and as good examples to farmers to do likewise. The Burlington and Missouri River Railroad had a large land grant and an active land agency at the time and was using advertising, farm extension, and agricultural experiment to encourage settlement and stimulate traffic.[9]

Two of the largest and most influential prairie experiments were catalpa plantations established near Farlington, Kansas, by H. H. Hunnewell. Hunnewell, a Massachusetts businessman, was president of the Kansas City, Fort Scott and Memphis Railroad Company, now part of the Frisco lines (St. Louis and San Francisco). The railroad planted an entire section (640 acres), and Hunnewell had a section of his own planted. Nearly half the land was planted to catalpa, the rest to various species, ailanthus (tree of heaven), white ash, osage orange, black walnut, and black cherry. A few trees were set in 1877, and the rest were contracted between 1879 and 1884 to the nursery of Robert Douglas and Sons. The catalpa and osage orange grew well and were thinned in 1894–1895. The prospects of tie production still looked very good at that time. This Farlington Forest was the inspiration and the evidence most frequently cited by private promoters of catalpa for railroads and public promoters of prairie planting between 1900 and 1910.[10]

Persistent efforts by the Saint Paul and Pacific Railroad, now part of the Great Northern, from 1871 to 1877 produced four million trees in windbreaks and snow fence plantations along the line through the southern Minnesota prairie. Contract planting, use of cuttings, sowing of acorns, mowing and burning, and plow cultivation were all tried. The railroad's example did much to encourage planting by settlers. It made available cheap cuttings and young trees. The land was improved and its value enhanced. The successful manager of the operation, Leonard Hodges, published a *Forest Tree Planter's Manual* which went through many editions and had considerable influence in prairie planting for fifteen or twenty years. He recognized the peculiarity of the incentives to plant by recommending cottonwood for a "tree claim." "It is a peculiar freak of nature that the most worthless timber is of easiest propagation, the hardiest in its nature, and of the most rapid growth." [11] Like other arboriculturists, he believed that planted forests would moderate the local climate, and in his calculations of returns, he figured no interest.

These railroad experiments were, in general, considered successful. By using land accounted free or surplus, by charging no interest on the investment, and by establishing intangibles as the chief benefits to be realized—public example, shade, wind protection—it was possible to consider the plantations as thoroughly beneficial and profitable.

Broadening the Idea of Forestry

The prairie experience was influential in creating a concern about forests in America. It was also influential in putting the popular emphasis on planting, particularly the planting of a few fast-growing hardwood species in the treeless regions. (The Europeans depended heavily on plantations, but the expected rotations were much longer, and they were planting native softwoods in regions of natural forest.)

A small group of persons interested in forestry were, however, gradually broadening their conception to include management. As they accumulated information about consumption and economic conditions, they borrowed and created a greater variety of forestry theories and solutions, and they placed new emphasis on utilization. This evolution was largely the work of the foresters in the Department of Agriculture. The new breadth of ideas began to dominate the forestry congresses and periodicals only in the 1890s.

The American Association for the Advancement of Science obtained the appointment of Franklin B. Hough as Forester of the United States, and the Department of Agriculture published his first *Report upon Forestry* in 1876. Hough established the first good estimates of U.S. timber consumption. He collected price information, studied plantings and other forestry activities in several states, and documented the timber thefts or "depredations" on public lands under the care of the Department of the Interior. In every aspect of forest problems—purchases, thefts, plantings—the railroads played a significant role.

Although practically no funds were provided for action during the 1870s, Hough set forth for his successors the peculiar conditions of American forestry. One contribution was his rational view of prairie arboriculture. He stated in his first report that 16 percent of the prairie land claims under the timber culture acts had already been canceled by September 1877 for conflict, relinquishment, or abandonment. "From somewhat extended personal inquiries we are led to believe that the proportion will eventually be found much larger—in many districts 50 per cent or even more, it being evident that in many cases the claims are held merely for speculative purposes, or were entered without appreciating the task undertaken. In fact, the requirements of the law are such that a man must have some considerable means in order to fully meet the requirements, and such men can often do better with their capital of money and labor than to seek its benefits." [12] Obviously he did not discourage the prairie planting enthusiasts, who were even more zealous in the 1880s.

Hough's immediate successor, Nathaniel Egleston, contributed less new thinking, but documented forest fires with care. Here again the railroads played a part; this time they were definitely villains, scattering sparks through the countryside.[13] The railroads were vulnerable in public opinion because of their behavior as local monopolies and their unpopular image as big business against the common man.

Bernhard E. Fernow, appointed "Chief of the Division of Forestry" in the Department of Agriculture in 1888, firmly established "depletion" as the keystone in the American forestry bureaucracy and the American public conscience.

Our forest resource was, in his view, being rapidly depleted, and commercial catastrophe would eventually result. Nevertheless, in his ten years in the position Fernow developed the American conception of forestry along new lines. He made it broader, more realistic, more professional, and more sophisticated. He introduced European, especially German, know-how and training in certain areas of timber utilization and engineering. But he recognized that European-style forestry could not be applied in the United States under current conditions of supply. It would first be necessary to reduce further the supply of virgin timber and establish "the fact of a threatened scarcity." [14] Meanwhile, he devoted two-thirds of his tiny appropriation for forestry (about 1 percent of the Department of Agriculture budget) to research in wood technology and spreading this information to the consumers of wood.

It is possible to infer from his annual report of 1893 that depletion propaganda was more or less consciously linked to depletion of the division's finances. Fernow made rough estimates of a thirty-year supply of timber in the nation and carried on a public argument with the Geographer of the United States, Henry Gannett, whom he accused of exaggerating the supply of timber in the Pacific Northwest. Neither had much information. A later comment of Fernow's in his own magazine shows the relation between the idea of depletion and the growth of professionalism in forestry: "It behooves, then, every forester, to find justification for his art and for his own existence in the answer to the inquiry which will bring out the fact that natural supplies are waning, and are not being replaced as fast as consumed." [15]

From 1866, when Andrew Fuller published a full-blown theory of commercial tree planting, to the 1890s, when Fernow was Forester, public concern about the forests grew. It was probably influenced more profoundly by the psychology of forest destruction, by European example, and by the unique prairie settlement experience than by actual consumer experiences of shortage, but the consumers, such as the railroads, were caught up in the drama. The expectation of national timber famine became general.

Throughout that period, there was, however, increasing divergence of opinion about the actions that should be taken. There were two somewhat different views of forestry in the U.S. by the 1890s. There was the popular interest in prairie planting. At the same time there was a smaller, more sophisticated group of men interested in European forest management and wood technology. They questioned the value of prairie planting, or at least its value as a panacea, but they too feared depletion and sought to "sell" their more varied package of remedies to the public.

Railroad men promoted both approaches. Men like Hunnewell and Hodges—one a railroad president, the other an employee—contributed to the enthusiasm for prairie planting. The railroads practiced it more successfully and more genuinely than anyone else. On the whole, the railroad experimenters were pleased with their efforts, but railroad men did not limit themselves to planting experiments. They cooperated closely with Foresters Hough and Fernow in broadening the base of information and ideas. Again in cooperation with Fernow, they considered a great variety of possible alternatives, including changes in their ways of using wood.

Chapter 4

"Let It Rot in the Good Old Way"

The apprehension expressed in popular magazines, scientific journals, public congresses, and the daily press infected businessmen as well. The response of commerce and industry was the instinctive one of self-defense. The first line of defense was change within the firm, the unit over which the individual businessman had some control. He prepared to modify his own production to use resources more efficiently. The general cry of alarm triggered research and development which would make technical changes possible if and when a crisis came. However, the alarmists failed to foresee such modifications of resource uses, the normal responses of "economic man." They continued to predict a crisis after technical solutions had been sketched.

Technical improvement meant greater efficiency. With more knowledge and better organization, the same job could be done with fewer total resources. Or, the same job could be done with less of one particular resource and more of another, adding up to no greater total cost. Between 1875 and 1895 American railroad men recognized this and forged tools of research, development, and communication that they would bring to bear on timber problems.

In the development of tools of railroad science, the process of railroad consolidation was crucial. Railroad consolidation occurred in the 1870s and 1880s by means of pools, leases, holding operations, purchases, and mergers. The Burlington system was typical. On the Burlington the consolidation of the early 1880s resulted in drastic changes in purchases, stores, and materials economy between 1887 and 1891. To harmonize procedures on the several lines, T. H. Leavitt, a consultant, visited all the storehouses and examined their accounts. Comparison revealed economies that could be applied throughout the system. For example, the lumber dealer who supplied two or three points was not providing the same value because of variations of inspection practices. The various systems of lumber grading on the lines had to be reconciled. Leavitt observed the habitual overstocking of lumber and recommended reforms to control inventory. In order to stock a smaller number of articles, the railroad established lists of "standard items" and created specifications for standard sizes of lumber.[1] Cleanup of lumberyards reduced losses from decay. Leavitt found storekeepers were only accounting for values in their invoices and inventories. He recommended accounting of quantities to obtain rates of use and to determine reasonable inventories.

Consolidation on the Burlington permitted the discovery of more efficient methods. Opportunities for savings were greater for the larger firm: for example, consolidation made possible economies of large-scale purchasing in a wider market, and it permitted economies of integrated operation such as the supply of hardwood engine kindling and fence posts from carshop and track department scrap.

The lessons learned on the Burlington, the New York Central, and other major railroad systems consolidated in the 1880s influenced the thinking of railway engineers. The experience of consolidation and its rewards encouraged the creation of institutions and methods for collecting information and analyzing economic problems on the railroads as a whole. In 1899, for example, the railway engineers of many systems formed a professional organization—the American Railway Engineering Association (AREA)—which was a forum for collecting and comparing statistics and accounts of railroad systems, analyzing new techniques, and hammering out industry-wide standards. AREA and its sister societies extended the defense mechanisms of the firm to the entire industry.

Thus the railroads prepared themselves for flexible responses to changing economic conditions through efficient research, development, and sharing of new technology. The research and communications tools or defenses were not created in response to the specific threat of timber famine. But, thanks to their new institutions, as the railroads grew concerned about a possible shortage of timber, they were able to apply new approaches to that particular set of engineering problems.

The major opportunities for improved utilization of wood were of three types: to substitute, in certain uses, new materials for old, either new species or grades of wood or entirely different materials such as steel and concrete; to improve design in order to build structures that could withstand the same stresses, but with smaller amounts of wood; to make wood last longer by chemical preservation.

All these opportunities required some substitution of capital, more labor, or some other resource for wood. Change also involved some risk. Consequently, changes were not likely to be sought unless there was a prospect of rising timber prices. Once discovered, changes were not likely to be effected until timber prices did rise. The alarm of 1875–1895 induced research and development, but because timber prices to the railroads were considered stable throughout this period, innovations were not economic. Most of the production changes that were discovered were not put into practice in the period before 1895, except under special local conditions.

Materials Research

Advances in knowledge of the properties of materials made it possible to substitute cheaper grades and kinds of timbers in many uses and to substitute materials such as concrete and steel for timber. Great advances were made in this branch of technology during the 1890s. Though the applications were scarcely perceptible, their potential was enormous.

The principal stimulus to materials research was the demand for steel, especially steel rail. Railroad research on steel rail contributed in many ways to the technology that later permitted efficient use of wood and substitution of other materials for wood.[2] As equipment grew heavier and traffic more frequent, rail renewals loomed larger in railroad expenses, and the railroads began tests to discover which rails would give longest service. Steel rail could be manufactured with a far greater degree of control and to a greater variety of standards than the old iron rail. Therefore, the railroads experimented to establish the ideal specifications and tested to guarantee that manufacturers were meeting those specifications. Each large railroad system began its own testing program. The Burlington, for example, founded a central testing laboratory in 1876 at the same time that the line adopted Bessemer steel rail. Analyses were shared among railway engineers who were a strong contingent in the American Society of Civil Engineers (ASCE). The interest in steel rail was a first concern of the AREA and the chief reason for participation of railway engineers in founding the American Society for Testing Materials (ASTM; 1899).

The handling of rail problems set a pattern that was later applied to crossties. Railroad men used and developed chemical analysis, microscopic study, physical tests, and statistical methods in their attempt to obtain longer lasting rail. They devised laboratory and manufacturing tests that would identify defective rails before they were put in track. It was no coincidence that Paul Dudley of the New York Central, one of the pioneers in this work, also made the first photomicrographs relating wood structure to strength of ties and preservative treatment. He identified several of the fungi that cause decay of ties in track.[3]

The advance of laboratory analysis was important, but service records were the ultimate test. Beginning in 1884 the Burlington kept elaborate records of performance of rails. In 1887 its engineers compiled from the records a set of Rail Failure Tables. These tables, recalculated semiannually, were diagrams of location, manufacture, date of placement, and physical and chemical characteristics of all rail in track and the number failed (replaced). They provided the data for analysis of variance. Railroads that preserved ties were the first to keep crosstie records, and their method followed precisely the pattern of the rail records. Systems of records for tie renewals and test tracks after 1900 were all abbreviated from the rail records. The steel rail problem also demanded engineering attention to track stresses. Attempts to measure strains and theorize about track structure subsequently contributed to the solution of railway timber problems.

International organizations provided a stimulus for American materials research of a broader kind. In 1896 the American Society of Mechanical Engineers established a Committee on Methods of Testing Materials to cooperate with the International (European) Commission. This was the nucleus from which an ASTM grew. American engineering schools began to train their students in the engineering science of materials. For example, J. B. Johnson at Washington University, St. Louis, assisted in timber physics tests and in 1897 published an influential textbook on the properties of materials. This text reported European findings and brought together data from American tests. Johnson was concerned with the development and standardization of machinery and methods for testing materials of all kinds. He attempted to relate empirical work to theoretical conceptions and to determine the engineering relations between cost and strength in the economy of materials. "Rational design involves knowledge of (1) the external forces to be resisted, transformed, or transmitted, (2) the internal stresses resulting, and (3) the mechanical properties of the materials employed . . . The first two are founded on the sciences of mathematics and applied mechanics, the last one, however, does not rest on any deductive science, as this information can be gained only by patient, expensive, and competent research . . . The idea of mechanical testing is to standardize, so as to permit theoretical and scientific generalizations and repeatability, and to grade materials for purposes." [4]

Municipalities also showed an interest in testing materials in order to design building codes and to require fire-resistant construction.

The most important stimulus to American timber testing was the geographical expansion of the wood markets owing to the transport improvements of the 1870s and 1880s. Species that were formerly sold in a local market were now offered to consumers in regions that had traditionally used other local species. The substitution of wood species for one another became economically attractive as a result of the compensating changes in supply described in Chapter 2: the depletion of local supplies and the expanding supply of timbers from further away.[5]

The first orderly series of tests on American woods was made for Sargent's report on American forests to the Bureau of the Census in 1881.[6] Substitution to alleviate local shortages was one objective, but a more important one was to estimate the value for economic development of the more remote forested regions that were now becoming accessible. Sargent's series of tests on small selected specimens did not, however, add much to the understanding of wood structure or engineering principles.

The most important tests were the Timber Physics series of forty thousand tests directed by Fernow during his tenure as Chief of the Division of Forestry in the 1890s. Fernow promoted testing in part because he feared depletion and believed that there could be 20 or 25 percent economy of wood use by selection of species for appropriate uses, and another 25 percent economy in the proper seasoning of wood to develop its full strength. His selection of subjects shows that he understood the problems posed to consumers by the expansion of supply through transport. The first group of timbers tested were the southern pines, whose classification created problems for railroads and other users in distant markets. He paid special attention to bridge timbers which moved the longest distances into the widest markets (fig. 10). He was interested in railroads not only because they were such large consumers, but because they were efficiency-conscious consumers and had access to wider markets than, say, the average domestic user of firewood.

The Timber Physics tests were carried on with the closest attention to new methods of materials testing. Fernow's concern with the properties and economics of wood was characteristic of the most progressive engineering thinking of the time. Consequently, the tests contributed to the general

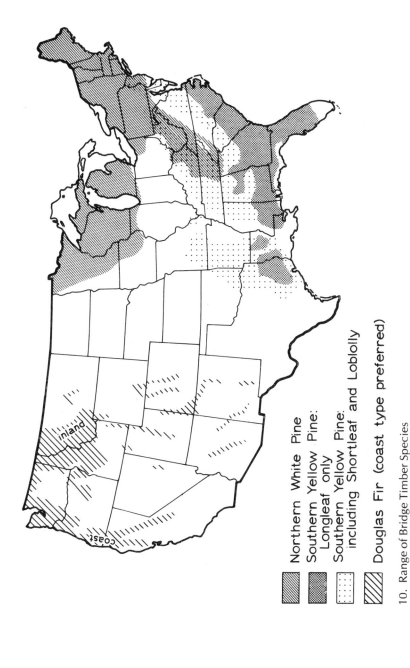

Northern White Pine

Southern Yellow Pine:
Longleaf only

Southern Yellow Pine:
including Shortleaf and Loblolly

Douglas Fir (coast type preferred)

10. Range of Bridge Timber Species

49

understanding of the engineering properties of wood as well as of the properties of certain species.

The simplest type of result was the demonstration that one species was perfectly interchangeable with another. For example, in 1887 Fernow showed that chestnut oak (*Quercus montana*) was as strong as white oak (*Quercus alba*). Formerly disdained, chestnut oak was adopted by several railroads for crosstie use. Gradually, the "white oak group" of species, including chestnut oak and post oak, were accepted as of equal value with the white oak tie. Shortly after this, studies of southern pines demonstrated that bleeding trees for turpentine in no way damaged the strength of the timber. Trees that had been bled for many years were therefore no longer excluded from the bridge timber market. Substitutions such as this, which increased local supply, merely required information to overcome unfounded prejudices. Later substitutions would require more investment and more radical changes in practice.

The tests demonstrated the importance of air seasoning of timber. Seasoning or drying wood permits development of full strength, but seasoning by boiling, steaming, or dry heat may injure wood. Seasoning also reduces the probability of decay if the wood is subsequently protected from dampness. The relation between seasoning and strength of wood made it important to control the moisture content of the timbers used in the tests. Fernow's most important contribution was comprehension of the complex system of variables involved in timber testing. "This endless variability it is that has kept us in ignorance as to the capabilities of our timbers. We need a large number of specimens of known origin [to control the many variables] and known physical conditions [moisture control] . . . Timber Physics is the pivotal science of the art of Forestry."[7]

The tests established firm empirical relationships between

specific gravity of wood and its various engineering properties. For example, specific gravity was found to be related to cross-breaking strength and ultimate crushing strength. Ultimate strength in compression is related to the strength of a beam at the elastic limit. He studied the variability of large and small pieces: "A small beam is not proportionately [stronger]. A large timber generally gives values nearer the average, as it contains a larger quantity and greater variety of the wood of the tree. Average values derived from a large series of tests on small but representative material may be used in practice with perfect safety, and these averages are not likely to be modified by tests on large material." [8]

Generalized relationships such as the above made it possible to use simplified tests of sample materials to estimate properties of new species. They also made it possible to formulate practical systems of grading large structural timbers, including the southern pines. The five southern pines studied were of indistinguishable structure. When moisture content was controlled by seasoning, the strength of any piece proved to vary in proportion to specific gravity and the ratio of dense summerwood to springwood. In the early 1900s manufacturers introduced a crude system of commercial grading based on this groundwork. The general relationships described also made possible improved engineering design of structures discussed below.

Since improved access continued to make wood available at low cost, few of Fernow's major practical recommendations were applied in the 1890s. Economizing wood was now possible through seasoning, species selection, and rational design, but there was little incentive. Fernow expected to see wood railroad ties replaced with steel. A Forestry Division bulletin boosted the idea and initiated a wave of patents and small-scale experiments.[9] Here again, the technology appeared, but it was not applied. Fernow also proposed research that would have given higher value to wood by developing its uses and controlling its properties. He proposed research on fire retardants, for example, electrical properties, and hygroscopic stabilization of wood.[10] His program of utilization was scrapped, however, when Congress diverted the funds in 1896 to tree planting on the plains; this led to his resignation in 1898.

Bridge Design

Rapid construction of railroads under the special conditions of the prairies had caused railroad companies to adopt the military bridge methods developed by Hermann Haupt during the Civil War. Construction engineers built wood pile trestles and sacrificed extra materials for speed of construction and economies of labor. Haupt sought efficiency of a special kind and did some testing because there was no tradition to rely on. His tests were very crude. No theory of distribution of stresses was employed, and no components were tested. Haupt simply built the bridge, loaded a car with railroad iron, and pulled it back and forth across the bridge with ropes. On each trial the load was increased. On some trials the load was allowed to stand for some hours, and the deflections were noted. Eventually the bridge collapsed. The breaking weight was recorded in pounds per linear foot of bridge.

In the 1870s and 1880s, however, the process of consolidation and standardization on the railroads affected bridge design as it had affected inventory, purchasing, and maintenance practices. Each large railroad system created standard plans that could be adapted easily to various spans and heights. These were modifications of the wood pile trestle and the common Howe truss bridge. Then the concept of standard bridge design was extended to groups of railroad systems. In 1895 the American Railway Bridges and Building Association published a report of a committee chaired by Walter Berg, of the Lehigh Valley Railroad. Berg calculated the working stresses that were actually being assumed for timbers and pointed out problem areas in bridge design, such as concepts of impact and safety factors.[11]

Interest in rational bridge design was stimulated by the fact that the lightly built timber structures of the prairie railroads of the 1870s and 1880s were now reaching the end of their service life, and railroads did not want to replace them with obsolete structures. Because more information had been accumulated on traffic, local stream behavior, and other design factors, the new structures would not need the same flexibility, and the so-called "permanent materials"—stone, steel, earthwork—could be used.

Meanwhile the general progress of metallurgy permitted more efficient design of steel bridges; the first large steel railroad bridge was built at St. Louis in 1873. Rapid progress was made toward cheaper designs in steel. Consequently, without important changes in the cost of timber, substitution of steel became attractive in the 1890s in the regions where timber had always been expensive. On the Chicago, Milwaukee and St. Paul Railway (6,150 miles), for example, bridge replacement began in 1888 with a change of management in the bridge department. Between 1888 and 1895 timber culverts were replaced at the rate of five hundred a year. About four-fifths of the replacements were of iron pipe, one-fifth of secondhand bridge timber. (In the "hard times" of 1893 the price of iron fell while the price of timber did not.) Railway management cited this favorable ratio as a reason for the replacement of wooden Howe trusses with iron structures. The cost differential was not sufficiently favorable to justify replacement of wood with iron trestles, but many trestles were replaced with earth embankments—one-fifth, or twenty-one miles of railroad, by 1895. In the same way, the Santa Fe railroad in the 1890s replaced thirty-five miles of wood bridges and a large proportion of culverts with "permanent materials." Few other railroads began substitution of this kind much before 1900. The choice between timber and iron or earthwork was influenced by changes in relative costs of structures of different materials, but the cost differentials resulted from the progress of design and use of materials. They did not result from any changes in unit prices that might have reflected tighter supply of some materials.

In 1896 A. L. Johnson in a *Bulletin* of the Division of Forestry proposed new designs for timber trestles. He emphasized potential savings of materials. On the evidence of reports from fifteen large railroads, and the study of Walter Berg, Johnson estimated that there were in 1896 more than 2,000 miles of timber trestle in the United States, valued at $60,000,000, probably twice the capital invested in iron and steel structures. The annual replacement of about one-ninth of the material consumed 260,000,000 board feet of timber and required the expenditure of about $7,000,000. Most of this timber was of large sizes and higher cost per board foot than small timbers.

Johnson claimed that eight hundred miles or two-fifths of those trestle bridges were designed with certain characteristic flaws. The vertical members (posts and piles) were designed for much heavier loads than the horizontal members (caps and stringers) could carry (figs. 11 and 12). Such design was the result of using average values for timber strength, when in fact timber has much greater endwise crushing strength than crushing strength across the grain. The bearing surfaces were not proportioned to the loads. The errors were also the result of empirical bridge construction such as Haupt's, where the several members were not designed and tested independently of the whole. Because a bridge was only as strong as its weakest members, many bridges were either overdesigned or

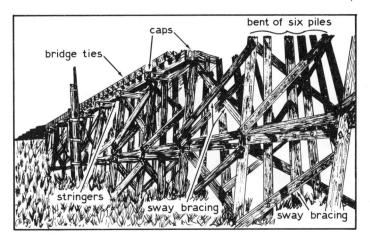

11. Trestle Structure

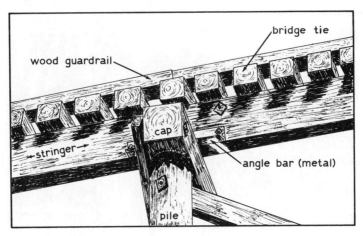

12. Details of Trestle Construction

overstressed, with consequent waste of wood and unnecessary limits on the species that could be employed.[12]

Bridge building was one of the branches of engineering in which the railroads achieved important advances between the Civil War and 1900. The progress of analytical methods, increase in empirical information, and growth of institutions for sharing knowledge created a reservoir of technical choices which would permit the railroads to respond to any change in prices.

Wood Preserving

The technology of preserving wood from rot by impregnating it with chemicals made rapid advances in Europe in the first half of the nineteenth century. Although the use of salt to discourage rot of vessels was ancient, and seasoning wood was known to prevent decay, the reasons were not understood. The decay of wood was recognized as an important naval problem; navies were, therefore, the first to employ the new and more efficient chemical preservative techniques, notably Kyan's (1832) and Boucherie's (1840) use of mercuric chloride (corrosive sublimate) in England and France, respectively. Small commercial ventures were founded in Europe, and the railways immediately showed an interest in preservation of crossties. The Burnett zinc chloride method was found to be effective and less dangerous to handle than mercury compounds. Creosote was known to be effective, but it was still too expensive to be used widely before 1850.

The new practices were founded on a theory which wrongly attributed decay to chemical changes which took place spontaneously when life ceased or "the vital principle" was removed. The chemical changes were called "coagulation of albumen," and the appearance of fungi on the decayed wood was considered a symptom. This theory of coagulation recog-

Track laying in September 1887 in Montana Territory, on the St. Paul, Minneapolis & Manitoba (later Great Northern, now Burlington Northern). Track-laying records of over eight miles a day were set, using large labor force, horses and wagons, and the simplest of tools. The ties vary in length.

Close-up of track laying in 1887, near Havre, Montana. Crossties were rough hewed, irregular in shape and thickness. Soldiers are from nearby Fort Assiniboine.

Timber seasoning and storage yard at the Burlington's wood-preserving plant, Sheridan, Wyoming, in the early 1900s. Built in 1902, this plant supplied crossties treated with zinc chloride for the construction of the western lines (shown below). The photo above shows the ties sawed to uniform size, stacked in open piles for air seasoning; and also timbers loaded on trams ready to be moved into the pressure-treating cylinder in the building.

Track-laying outfit used on the Burlington between 1907 and 1914 to build the line between Billings, Montana, and Casper, Wyoming, critical in the grand strategy of James J. Hill for connecting the Burlington, Northern Pacific, Great Northern, and the Colorado Southern. All are now part of the Burlington Northern.

Snow-bucking outfit on the Mosquito Creek bridge, Cascade Mountains, 1887, Northern Pacific railroad, now part of the Burlington Northern. Problems with drifting snow were the major reason for tree planting by the northern railroads. The water barrels shown here were to douse sparks. By the turn of the century, the high multistory wood trestles were being replaced with "permanent" steel and earthwork. A few are now found, of creosoted timber, on secondary and branch lines in the Northwest. The long, low one-story trestles and "approaches" are still standard practice throughout the country.

Track laying in 1970 by the Morrison Knudsen Company in the relocation of fifty-nine miles of the Burlington Northern line near Libby, Montana. This tie-placing machine is followed by another giant machine which lays down ribbon rail, an autosled which raises the track and adds ballast, then tamper and liner machines. The project required 243,000 ties.

Tramloads of crossties are sealed into the pressure-treating cylinder at the wood-preserving plant in Paradise, Montana. Most ties are treated with solutions of coal tar creosote and petroleum.

One of the early catalpa plantations in Kansas, photographed in 1906, when the trees were twenty to thirty years old and over thirty feet tall. Because of their shape, branching, and defects, the "forest" produced fence posts only. For descriptions of four such groves, planted 1878–1892, see "The Hardy Catalpa," U.S. Department of Agriculture, Forest Service, *Bulletin* (No. 37, 1902). Nursery stock for all of these was supplied from Robert Douglas & Sons, Waukegan, Illinois.

nized that moisture and warmth played a role in decay, and it encouraged identification of fungi as indicators of decay. Consequently it was of some practical use.

It was established in the course of scientific controversy over spontaneous generation in the 1840s, however, that the fungi, living organisms, were the agents of decay, not mere symptoms. Railroad men and foresters began to revise their views after 1850, as the importance of microscopic organisms was revealed in agricultural chemistry and medicine. Wood preserving was then reinterpreted as an antiseptic process rather than a chemical reaction. The coagulation theory nevertheless persisted for many years among patent process wood preservers.

Only two minor experiments were recorded in the United States before 1850,[13] but at the time of the Civil War the American railroads began to experiment with wood preserving. The supply of ties was still limited to a local market. Because wood was expensive in the zones of old settlement around Boston, New York, and Philadelphia, and in the prairies, the railroads in those two regions were the experimenters. The Philadelphia, Wilmington and Baltimore Railroad burnettized ties in 1863. The Old Colony Railroad in 1865 erected a plant at Somerset, Massachusetts, to creosote bridge timbers. Several patented processes were introduced commercially, but most of them were short lived. The Reading Railroad tried treating ties with urine. In the prairies the Rock Island line used creosoted wood in a bridge in 1860, and in 1869 the Burlington had fifteen thousand hemlock ties treated with creosote. Treatment did not succeed in prolonging their life, however. Because unseasoned timber was used, they decayed at the center.[14] The Union Pacific, trying to obtain in haste three million ties from a region with no roads, no labor supply, and few trees, had to depend on low-grade river valley timber to build westward. Most of the ties were cottonwood, which decayed rapidly, and the railroad tried treating them by the Burnett process. Their treatment, at the rate of five hundred per day at Omaha, created a bottleneck in construction operations. As soon as the line was built west to Wyoming, the railroad began to use untreated softwood species from Rocky Mountain watersheds such as Medicine Bow, Laramie, North Platte, Green River, Henry's Fork, Black's Fork, and the Bear and Weber rivers.

In the 1870s small American commercial operations made it clear that, of the two major types of preservative treatment practiced in Europe, creosote treatments were more advantageous at points on the eastern and Gulf coasts, and the metallic salt processes were more economical inland. Most railroads were not convinced, however, that treatment of any kind would produce economies for them under the current conditions of timber abundance.

Creosote was the only substance effective against the marine boring animals or worms such as the teredo which attacked piling in saltwater harbors. Creosote experiments were conducted by the U.S. Navy from 1872 to 1880. Both creosote and the metallic salts were effective against rot, but the salts were relatively more effective in dry climates and dry sites where the salt was not rapidly leached from the wood.

At least four railroads of the Atlantic and the Gulf coasts experimented with the Bethell and Hayford creosote processes. Their operations concentrated on trestles and bridge timbers, piling, wharves, and docks rather than crossties.[15] Midwestern railroads experimented with various patented salt preservatives in the late 1870s. Thilmany's modification of the Boucherie method used copper sulphate. It was applied to crossties for use on northern Ohio and Indiana railroads. The Wellhouse "zinc-tannin" process[16] was introduced in St. Louis in 1879 and was adopted for bridge timbers by local railroads.

In 1881 wood preserving became standard practice for crossties on the Santa Fe, Union Pacific, and Rock Island lines. All were prairie lines that had to pay high prices for ties, and all used the Wellhouse process and preliminary steaming to season the wood. For most railroads, however, economies from wood preserving were not yet apparent. The Burlington, for example, inquired about burnettizing in 1883. They were considering treating hemlock ties with zinc chloride as an alternative to oak ties. A green hemlock tie on the Chicago dock cost twenty-four cents, treatment cost twenty-four cents, and distribution on the line added a variable amount, so that the total cost in track would average fifty-four cents in Illinois and Iowa and sixty cents west of the Missouri River. Oak ties could be purchased for the same prices. The Burlington did not make a serious estimate of the life to be expected from a treated softwood tie as information was limited, but the expectation was that it would certainly not be greater than that of an untreated oak tie, about eight years.

The most important advance in wood preservation in America was the 1885 report of a special committee of the American Society of Civil Engineers. The committee studied the subject for five years. Important members were Octave Chanute (chairman), better known for his later interest in flight, and J. W. Putnam, manager of Gulf coast plants that treated bridge timber. Information was obtained from 2,350 people. The work was founded on the fear of depletion of the wood supply based on local experiences. This attitude was influenced by the Hough reports on forestry and by statements at the Montreal Forest Congress, which reported: "Even before the gathering of statistics on forestry for the census of that year [1880], it had become evident to engineers, from the increasing price and growing difficulty in procuring good timber, lumber and railroad ties in many parts of the United States, that several of the sources of such supplies were being rapidly exhausted, and that as a measure of both private and national economy it would soon become necessary for us to resort to the artificial preparation of wood against decay, as had been successfully done for years in Europe." [17]

The report compiled, translated, and made accessible the European technology of wood preserving, especially creosoting, a development of the last twenty-five years.[18] The analysis of American experience transformed that hodgepodge of unrelated tests into a document from which it was possible to demonstrate sound principles of treatment. The committee adopted the latest theory of wood preservation (antiseptic treatment to kill or prevent the growth of fungi and marine borers) and rejected the theory of coagulation of albumen.

The report emphasized the following principles. Pressure treatment is essential; merely steeping the wood is not effective. Sapwood and the sappy or porous species formerly disdained for structural uses are most easily treated and should be preferred where wood is to be preserved. It is necessary to consider both the use and environment for timber when planning treatment; different treatments are desirable for marine use, freshwater wet sites, and dry climates. Some seasoning is required. Artificial seasoning by steaming was condoned (most of the techniques practiced in the U.S. in the 1880s were processes involving high temperatures and included steaming).

An important feature of the report was its close attention to economic conditions. Differences between European and American timber markets were pointed out. The report concluded that, with the exception of marine use, there were few situations in the U.S. in which creosoting of ties would be profitable. "If the exposure is to be that of a railroad tie, creosoting is doubtless the most perfect process to use; but in view of the expense, it may be preferable to use a cheaper process, dependent somewhat upon the location, as away from the seaboard creosote is not available, and transportation is expensive." [19]

Economic analysis also made it clear that conditions were changing: "So long as wood was cheap, the cost of efficient preparation, including interest on plant and price of antiseptics, was so great in proportion to the ruling timber prices twenty or thirty years ago that timber preservation did not pay. It was cheaper to let it rot in the good old way . . ." [20] Accounts demonstrated that preservation would pay, if and when the price of ties rose. The method devised by the committee to estimate the cost in place of ties is essentially that used today. It took into account the interest on the investment and the desire of railroad managers to obtain immediate returns. The committee recommended treating the cheaper species which could thus be made to outlast the best woods in their natural state. The committee also recognized the American conditions of rapid construction and cyclical investment as restrictions on the value of treatment. Haste was the cause of failure in many of the preservative experiments of the American railroads: "The pressure was applied to the operatives instead of to the cylinder."

Very little progress in wood preserving occurred in the U.S. for about fifteen years after the American Society of Civil Engineers report was published. In 1903 Paul Dudley, who had been present at the discussions of 1885, stated at another meeting, "Eighteen years ago all the information was already in the world and could have been applied." [21] Why was the information not applied? Economic conditions did not justify the practice of wood preserving. Threats of change justified giving it some thought, but even a prairie line like the Burlington, which paid relatively high prices for wood, decided in 1883 against chemical treatment of ties and bridge timber. It also decided against rail chairs (metal plates to protect ties) and against the substitution of iron for wood in car construction. In the 1880s and 1890s large railroads like the Burlington were making large investments and many innovations. They were realizing real economies in maintenance of way, through purchasing and quality control, and they created a reservoir of new techniques for shortages that might occur. But so far greater overall economy did not imply much actual saving in the volume of wood they used. Wood was too cheap. It was so cheap, in fact, that prominent railway engineers ridiculed the idea of depletion during the discussion of the report at the 1885 meeting of the society. A. M. Wellington, a well-known railway economist, questioned whether it was a public advantage "to have timber over cheap" since wood structures created a fire hazard, and the U.S. used three to four times as much wood per capita as other countries. ". . . we find that we have an enormous area where timber will grow freely, and that our supply of timber is sufficient, with ordinary preservation and care, to answer all purposes, to give all the timber we really need. If timber gets high in price, people will use brick or stone and be more comfortable as well as more safe." [22] Charles Latimer of the New York, Pennsylvania, and Ohio Railroad ridiculed the depletion idea:

> Every one was expecting that the whales would give out and there would be no oil, and all of a sudden more oil was found than we could use. You remember Rankin wrote a paper: "What Shall We Do for Coal in England?" and now they have found that they have abundance of coal. In Wyoming Valley, where they had a good deal of black coal, the question arose finally, "What are we going to do for cheap coal; it is giving out?" Well, in the Pittsburgh region they have opened up immense gas fields. The next question was, "What are we going to do for steel?" and we are making it now as cheaply as iron. And now the question arises, "What are we going to do for hoop-poles?"

But iron is used for hoops almost universally. As to the question of building houses, Mr. Wellington spoke of everything but aluminum. We will have aluminum houses after awhile or some other metal, and not be bothered with wood. I think the trouble of cutting the forests is very much like killing the bears or killing the buffaloes. If you give up cutting timber for 50 years, the whole country will be overrun with forests, and the question will be how to get rid of them. The question is not yet serious.[23]

"Sentimentalism Joins Hands with Commercialism"

Expectations of the future naturally have their roots in experience of the past. In a business system geared to growth and structural change, managers pay most attention to recent experience and tend to discount the more distant past. Until World War I economic conditions of the interval 1895–1907 were critical in determining the expectations of resource managers and railroad managers. During this period railroad traffic was growing. Although maximum axle loads did not increase (about 60,000 to 65,000 pounds since 1890), many more heavy trains were operating on main lines, at higher average speeds. Research on steel rails began to pay off, and from 1893 expenditures for rail fell relative to expenditures for other materials.

Beginning in 1896 tie and timber prices began to rise, although they varied widely among regions. Tie renewals now represented outlays larger than any other item of railroad expense except labor and fuel. Any small change in tie prices or rate of tie renewals had, consequently, a large effect on total operating expenses. On the Santa Fe, for example, the annual maintenance of way budget in the late 1890s averaged a million dollars a year for tie renewals, a million dollars for bridge repairs (materials and labor), and half a million for rail renewals. Until 1907 the price of wood continued to rise.[1] Prices of other materials such as cement and steel fell, and the general price and wage level was fairly stable. The two factors in the rising price of timber were higher prices for stumpage (that is, standing timber in the woods) and higher freight bills paid for longer hauls.

After the financial crash of 1907, tie prices did not fall, but prices of cement and steel continued to fall relative to other items. Railroad wages did not vary much, although wage rates in other industries rose.

The experience with that set of variables was the "data" from which scientists and businessmen derived their expectations of the immediate future. The data had to be interpreted, or explained, in order to make projections into the future. The Forest Service elaborated an influential theory of wood prices. Railroad men based their expectations of these prices on their recent experience and on the Forest Service interpretation. By 1914, however, some inconsistencies appeared between the experience and the theory, and the "tie question" became controversial.

The Forest Service Interpretation

The view of the Forest Service was essentially that decreasing supply was causing wood prices to rise; that is, rising prices indicated depletion of supply. There were no satisfactory direct observations of physical supply available to evaluate this belief, and today's tools of econometrics were not at hand to analyze economic supply. Depletion was inferred from rising prices and from certain theoretical assumptions which we may call the physical requirements theory of resources. Foresters regarded supply as a naturally given physical quantity of timber of certain quality and size, and demand as a quantity consumed per capita regardless of price. Supply and demand were not understood as schedules or functions relating price to volume, and there was no attempt to estimate any price elasticity of supply or demand. As supply was consumed (depleted) by harvesting more than nature produced each year, the price would rise, but the same quantities would be required, and cutting would continue to reduce supply.

The interpretation of demand as a fixed requirement made supply the critical variable that determined price. Physical supply became the primary concern of the Forest Service when Gifford Pinchot became Chief in 1898. The assumptions and the inferences are illustrated in statements of the Forest Service between 1900 and 1909. "We have never been so near to the exhaustion of our lumber supply . . . The available supply of timber for railroad ties is rapidly dwindling away, and therefore it grows more important every day to find a cheap and still abundant material." [2] "The forests of the private owners will have to be set in order if the overwhelming calamity of a timber famine is to be kept from this nation." [3] Pinchot recommended holding loblolly pine as a permanent investment for producing tie timber.

I have never been able to reach a satisfactory estimate, taking the country at large, of what an acre of forest would produce in ties. But the fact remains even if we are not able to reach statistics of that sort—and such statistics, if they were obtained, would be of little use, because we do not know with any accuracy what is the supply of standing timber in the United States,—the fact remains that all the information we can get goes to prove that the total supply of timber is diminishing very rapidly and that the total consumption immensely exceeds the natural growth . . . Prices of timber are certain to increase with great rapidity. So far, therefore, as I am able to see, the only possible safety for the railroads lies in setting aside lands already their own, or lands which they themselves will buy, and devoting them, under the principles of practical forestry, to the production of their own timber supply.[4]

When wood and stumpage prices ceased to rise after 1907, it was necessary to elaborate the theory. There was no reason to believe that facts of physical supply had changed. The conclusions of the experience of 1900–1907 were that the cut exceeded the growth, and the existing body of theory said that supply was the determining factor in price. Then why did prices not continue to rise? The new principle was a step theory. Wood prices rose not gradually, but in jumps, as particular regional supplies were cut out. The exhaustion of timber in one region forced consumers to take their timber from a more remote region, and therefore to pay a higher price. The price then remained at the new level until the new regional supply was cut out. The expectation remained of severe shortage, rapid depletion of the entire national timber resource, further price rises, and dire effects on the cost of living. Any change in prices could be explained by this theory and would reinforce it. Ernest Bruncken formulated the best exposition:

In extractive forestry, transportation constitutes the greater portion of the whole expense . . . and furnishes reasons why forestry has a tendency toward monopolization . . . Consequently, compared with wheat, lumber prices are more or less local prices.

Chapter 5

Especially in a rapidly developing country . . . accessibility improves simultaneously with the increased demand, quite apart from any effort of the lumbermen themselves. Therefore, prices within a market district depending on extractive methods will often not rise very much, for a long time . . .

Knowledge of the amount of timber available is usually very vague, and therefore the supply is under- or over-estimated as it suits each person's interest or mental habit.

In extractive conditions, periods of very abrupt and considerable rise must alternate with periods of substantially stable and even falling prices. For every time a new level has been reached, large bodies of natural timber become accessible, whose exploitation was theretofore impossible on account of high transportation charges.[5]

Bruncken, a professor at the Yale School of Forestry, introduced a great many other elements into his explanation and does not seem to have been responsible for the way in which this particular idea was used.[6] Forest Service publications of 1907 and 1908 showed circular reasoning, overemphasis on the supply variable, and the projection of physical trends into the future. The price theory was no longer a hypothesis subject to modification or rejection as new evidence appeared, but a dogma.

That the decrease [in the hardwood cut, of 15 percent between 1899 and 1906] is due to diminished supply rather than to lessened demand seems to be proved beyond question.

If it is true that the hardwood supply is approaching a condition of shortage . . . then it is important to seek diligently the best means to avert it . . . but one practicable solution . . . a sufficient area under a proper system of forestry . . . Our experience will doubtless be the same in this respect as that of Germany.

Only within the last eight years have prices begun to reflect the dwindling supply, though the immoderate cutting away of this resource has been going on for decades.[7]

In another publication of the Forest Service, Raphael Zon asserted that the increasing population, growing need for agricultural land, and the demand for timber all over the world required increases in the productivity of forest land and reduction of waste. In line with this, he urged rigid supervision of tie makers to save wood and increase the revenue per acre; he did not consider the added cost of labor.[8]

In keeping with the depletion theory and the conviction that supply was critical, the Forest Service turned its attention away from forest products research and concentrated on silviculture (growing wood). Pinchot, in contrast to Fernow, believed European forestry practices could be applied in the United States *now*. His objective was public control of the means of production—the forest land. This would permit fire protection and the regulation of cutting and forest reproduction. In the first three years of his administration Pinchot devoted his entire budget to silviculture. A large part was spent on "working plans" for private forest owners. Nothing was known about setting up working plans, except the European rules, but Pinchot's slogan was "Forestry in the Woods," and for the present he refused to use the laboratory, the accounting office, or the research plot. Research was practically eliminated in the first few years of his administration, except for observations of the growth rates of trees and compilation of fire damages. The first was done with the stated purpose of proving that silviculture was profitable, and the second as propaganda for fire protection, "to ascertain the progress of the loss they cause." Publications were redirected toward those who might grow wood or form public opinion: farmers, capitalists, and the general public. Fernow's mailing list of two thousand engineers and technical men who used wood was extended by Pinchot to six thousand, including two thousand newspapers.[9]

One objective was to create a profession of forestry and to justify the profession. Another was to transfer control of the forestlands from the Department of the Interior to the Bureau of Forestry in the Department of Agriculture. In 1905 the bureau acquired control of the National Forests, and, from that time on, the tendency was to devote most of the personnel and budget to administrative problems. The bureau "has become to the people of the U.S. the recognized source of help in the handling of timber tracts and woodlots, the making of forest plantations, the study of commercial trees, and the investigation of important forest problems. It is occupying more and more fully its natural position as adviser in all forest matters in this country." [10]

It quickly became necessary, however, in response to the clamor of engineers (railway, civil, and mechanical) gradually to reinstate work on forest products technology. A Branch of Products was created. In 1902 the timber tests were begun again, actually carried out in the Bureau of Chemistry laboratory. In 1904, 12 percent of the bureau's budget was devoted to products work, and the achievements were even greater because the railroads, telephone companies, and other industries financed many projects, notably $20,000 a year for the work of von Schrenk at the Mississippi Valley Laboratory in St. Louis. The bureau invested $10,000 in a pilot plant for wood preserving at the St. Louis Exposition in 1904. Products work was justified in 1905 as contributing to forestry by assisting utilization of wood, that is, by reducing waste and making "conservative practices" pay. Tests of western species were expanded. Forest products research, like contemporary research in structural materials and plant industry, was carried on at decentralized stations in universities.[11] In 1906 a move began to centralize the work. Pressure from the railroads was helpful in obtaining a central laboratory, and the work on railway engineering at the University of Wisconsin influenced the selection of Madison, Wisconsin.[12] The new facilities offered by the university were to cost $50,000, but the equipment was already in existence at the several testing stations. The laboratory was expected to operate with a $28,000 government payroll and to receive $25,000 annual contributions from industry to cover other expenses. It opened in 1910. In 1911 an Office of Wood Utilization was created in the Forest Service, to report statistics of consumption. No economic analyses were made. Despite these developments, by 1912 forest products work represented 4 or 5 percent of the total Forest Service budget. The service had expanded far more rapidly than the products branch.

The Railroad View

Railroad men first based their expectation of rising wood prices on the ten-year trend that they had observed. Like the foresters, they regarded the "tie question" as a supply problem. It loomed large in discussions at annual conventions of the AREA. In 1901 it was noted that, "The eastern and middle states roads are now finding it necessary to go farther each year to secure the valuable white oak ties, and that at the same time, the price is steadily increasing, indicating a growing scarcity of the supply. They will therefore make inroads on the timber considered less valuable for cross-ties . . . and hence the tie question is becoming of importance to all tie consumers . . . the Government Division of Forestry is already doing valuable missionary work in that line." [13]

A year later it was stated that "A study of the tie question would naturally start with the possible supply in the country; but this is a subject so vast and one on which so much data is absolutely necessary to anything like an exact conclusion, that the Committee felt indisposed to touch it. However, the vastness of the supply has not been as much in evidence of late, as an apparent shortage, resulting in changes in character of tie material and the sources from whence it is drawn . . ." [14]

The Committee on Ties of the AREA began a survey of consumption patterns in 1902, in order to show the need for a thorough investigation by the Bureau of Forestry. "In view of the great scarcity of tie timber in this country, with the corresponding increased cost," the committee in 1906 recommended 8-foot ties where 8½-foot ties would admittedly improve track.[15] It reported in 1907: "In view of the present condition of the tie supply and the possible future supply, it does not seem wise to adopt these sizes." [16] A New York Central engineer stated: "It is vain to prophesy, but I believe the prices of lumber and ties will soon be on an upward trend and will continue to advance equally as much during the ensuing twenty years, as they have in the past score of years. These advances will be due to natural causes . . ." [17]

A Pennsylvania Railroad maintenance of way committee in 1910 tabulated prices of ties to the line from 1905 to 1909; they found that the prices were rapidly increasing and attributed the change to the fact that ties could no longer be obtained along the line on the same division of the railroad where they were to be used. The committee expected that ties would eventually be obtained nowhere along the line. "It is but a matter of several generations until the total available supply of timber will be exhausted. The annual growth is so much less than the annual cut that very little help may be expected from this source . . . The great depletion of the forests is already reflected in the supply of ties . . . shown by the substitution of inferior forms and woods." [18] The report recommended forest planting, artificial ties of steel or concrete, and prolongation of the life of the present ties. The language reflected statements of the Forest Service about supply. Extreme predictions after 1908 were based wholly on Forest Service sources. For example, "The supply of even second grade hardwood for ties, at almost any price is practically exhausted. The demand for softwoods, such as Oregon or Douglas fir and longleaf yellow pine, is rapidly exhausting this supply. Within relatively a few years we will be obliged to depend on the poorer grades of softwood for our bridge decks. On account of the great demand and rapid exhaustion of the supply the cost of the timber will constantly increase." [19] Also, "As we are using 40 cubic feet of timber per capita annually, while the annual growth of the forests produces only 13 cubic feet per capita, or only one-third of the timber consumed is replaced by growth, it was estimated at the Fifth Conservation Congress that we will experience a scarcity of timber in 33 years unless proper measures are taken to prevent it." [20] Or, a railroad executive to an engineering association, [There are] "many here tonight who will live to witness the disappearance of the American forests." [21]

The conditions of rising prices and expectations of continued increases encouraged the railroads to promote and even practice forestry. The profitability of forestry depended chiefly on the expectation of high wood prices and short rotations of the tree crop, which would minimize interest charges. Interest on even the shortest rotations represented half the cost of plantation forestry or forest management. Between 1900 and 1910 railroad men were influential participants in the forestry movement, and many railroads made small experimental ventures in forest tree planting. They encouraged the work of the Bureau of Forestry and took advantage of its technical assistance program.

In January 1905 railroad presidents and managers played leading roles at the American Forestry Congress, convened to hasten the conveyance of the National Forests from the Department of the Interior to the Bureau of Forestry. Nineteen railroads were represented, together with telephone, telegraph, and mining companies—all the principal commercial consumers of forest products. Among the speakers were the top brass of the Pennsylvania and Burlington railroads and the respected railway bridge engineer Walter Berg. Charles F. Manderson, the general solicitor of the Burlington, described the forestry movement in these terms. "We should rejoice in the fact that in this movement fraught with so much good to the republic sentimentalism joins hands with commercialism." [22]

When in 1909 Pinchot developed the notion of conservation as applicable to all national resources, railroad men were again instrumental in organizing a National Conservation Congress which created the new public spirit. Railroad president L. F. Loree of the Baltimore and Ohio and A. S. Baldwin, chief engineer of the Illinois Central, called the meeting, and railway engineers and master mechanics (locomotive builders) were active in the appeal.[23]

Railroad Forestry

The map (fig. 13) and table show the railroads that planted trees during this period, with the acreages, species, and locations. Railway engineers, government foresters, and conservation publications devoted much attention to these small projects because few other private forestry operations were attempted. Their significance is great because govern-

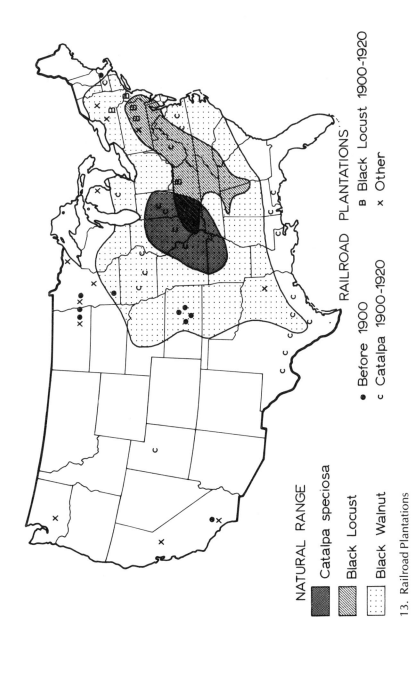

NATURAL RANGE

Catalpa speciosa

Black Locust

Black Walnut

RAILROAD PLANTATIONS

- Before 1900
c Catalpa 1900-1920
B Black Locust 1900-1920
x Other

13. Railroad Plantations

Table 2. Railroad forestry ventures, 1899–1914.

Dates	No. of Trees	No. of Acres	Species	Rail Line and Purposes
1898–1900	35,000		catalpa	Cleveland, Cincinnati, Chicago and St. Louis (Big Four), near Indianapolis, response to state tax incentive[b]
1900	65,000			Denver and Rio Grande Western, Provo Line[b]
1901	20,000	25	catalpa	Boston and Albany RR, near Westfield, Massachusetts[a]
1902	management	1,250,000		Kirby Lumber Co. and Houston Oil Co., southeast Texas, working plan USFS for management of reserved oil lands for railroad ties[c]
1900–1903	80,000	123	catalpa	Michigan Central, at section houses
1902				Oregon Railroad and Navigation Co., sand dune stabilization, along Columbia River
1902–1909	3,500,000		black locust	Pennsylvania Railroad in Pennsylvania[c,a]
1902–1903	110,000	450	catalpa	Illinois Central Railroad at Harahan, near New Orleans (250 acres), and Duquoin, Illinois, on coal mines (200 acres)[a]
1902	50,000		catalpa	Louisville and Nashville Railroad, near Pensacola, Florida

Year			Species	Railroad and location
1903–1906	2,000,000	1,000	catalpa, black locust	Louisville and Nashville Railroad, at Carney, Alabama, near Mobile (catalpa), East St. Louis, and Newport, Kentucky (black locust)[b,a]
1903	15,000		catalpa	Galveston, Harrisburg and San Antonio RR, between New Orleans and El Paso, Texas
1903–1928	management / 150,000	2,600	pine, larch, poplar, red oak	Delaware and Hudson Railroad, forests and nurseries in Adirondacks. Work expanded from plantings and nurseries to management of 12,500 acres, then 150,000 at maximum[c]
1905	thousands			Atchison, Topeka and Santa Fe, near Stockton, California[a]
1905	38,000	1,200	pine, black locust	Detroit and Mackinac RR, sand control, Tawas Beach, Michigan
1905	2,000	16	catalpa	Norfolk and Western RR, Ivor, near Tampico[b]
1906	thousands		catalpa	Mexican Central Ry., near Tampico[b]
1906	40,000		catalpa	Southern Railway, Wolf Trap, Virginia
1906	35,000	51	catalpa	Pennsylvania RR Lines West, near Kosciusko, Indiana[a]
1906		8	catalpa	Western Maryland RR, east of Elkins, West Virginia[b]
1906	100,000	115	catalpa	Chicago, Burlington and Quincy RR, Pacific Junction, Iowa[c]

Table 2. Railroad forestry ventures, 1899–1914 (continued).

Dates	No. of Trees	No. of Acres	Species	Rail Line and Purposes
1906–1907	94,000		yellow locust	Delaware, Lackawanna and Western, at Towaco, New Jersey, and Alden, New York[a]
1906–1912		200	yellow locust, red oak	Cumberland Valley RR[a]
1907–1909	3,000,000	8,825	eucalyptus	Atchison, Topeka, and Santa Fe RR, San Dieguito Ranch, near Del Mar, California.[c,a]
1907	hedge, 1 mile		barberry	Lake Superior and Ishpeming Ry.
1908	25,000	8	tamarack	Canadian Pacific RR, snow fences. The CP also held 600,000 acres of timber reserves[a]
1909	22,000		catalpa	San Antonio and Arkansas Pass RR, Skidmore, Texas[b]
before 1909	hedge		privet	Central Railroad of New Jersey, snow fence, $10 per hundred feet
1911–1914	management	30,000		Pennsylvania Railroad, extended management from 1,200 acres of cutover, to 30,000 acres by 1914[c]

Sources: [a] Proceedings, American Railway Engineering Association, XVI (1915). [b] John P. Brown, Practical Arboriculture (Connersville, Ind., 1906). [c] These plantations are mentioned in the text and indexed under the railroad name; miscellaneous sources are given in the notes.

ment forestry was concerned primarily with problems of land acquisition, fire control, measurement of physical growth, and propaganda. The Forest Service did little research on forest economics because government foresters were already committed to forestry as "profitable." [24] Private railroad forestry projects tested this supposition.

The railroad experiments were not all well designed, and many were influenced by amateur enthusiasts who made them pet projects which successors abandoned. American forestry was moving in the direction of forest management, as distinguished from plantation forestry, yet the railroad experiments of this period were chiefly plantations. In 1909, for example, the Forest Service was promoting selective cutting of natural loblolly pine stands in eastern Texas as a commercial tie forest, but meanwhile the Norfolk and Western Railway cleared, at great expense, fifteen acres in Virginia of "an excellent growth" of loblolly pine and planted catalpa trees on it. (The catalpa did not survive, and the experiment was discontinued.) The railroads did test a wide variety of species, soils, and methods of planting and cultivation. They invented tree-planting machines, and their rights-of-way constituted sample plots of varied climates.

The most influential projects were those of the Burlington, the Santa Fe, the Pennsylvania, and the Delaware and Hudson. The several projects and the expectations on which they were based are described first. The outcomes of the plantations are discussed later, since it was several years before expectations were modified. It is unfortunate that the railroad experiments lacked precisely what they might best have contributed—sensible accounting methods. As a result, the answers to questions about forest economics emerged slowly, and for many years opinions differed as to the success of some of the projects.

Between 1906 and 1921 the Burlington invested $24,000,

not including interest, in planting and tending 176,000 trees on 200 acres or more. The plantings were initiated as a pet project of J. D. Besler, a railroad man who had worked his way into top management and was retired to tend catalpa trees. His 1905 correspondence with John Pinckney Brown of Connersville, Indiana, shows the connection with the small but voluble group who promoted the "catalpa craze" nationwide. Besler enthusiastically had groves planted on every division, a few hundred to several thousand trees in a grove. The largest was about 100 acres. The record of changing expectations from this large grove at Pacific Junction, Iowa, reveals characteristics common to most of the railroad plantations.

The first plan, 1905, was for a tract of idle Burlington land along the Missouri River. No charges were made for land or interest on the investment. A tie crop was expected to mature in twenty years, and net returns were postulated (table 3). A report on the plantation after its first year allowed interest (at 5 percent) and land rent and still figured a net return. Critical assumptions were the twenty-year rotation, and the belief that subsequent crops would be produced on a fifteen-year rotation by means of stump reproduction and early rapid growth. Late in 1909 these calculations were revised to account for losses from hail, but because tie prices had risen and expectations of yield were extremely optimistic, calculations indicated a high net return.

In 1906–1907 the Santa Fe purchased exotic species for experimental ties. The tie and timber agent, E. O. Faulkner, brought timbers from Japan, the Philippines, and Hawaii, and five thousand ties of sixteen varieties of eucalypts from Australia. Six million seeds were imported, and the company established plantations of eucalyptus on 8,825 acres at San Dieguito, east of Del Mar, California. The land was cleared and harrowed, and the first seedlings were set in 1907 in the expectation that at the end of six years thinnings would be marketable for fence posts and cordwood. In 1910 expectations continued to be optimistic, although it had been necessary to install irrigation. In 1910 the Santa Fe anticipated cutting two hundred ties per acre, worth a dollar each, at the end of a twenty-year rotation.[25]

To reduce soil erosion and provide future crossties, the Pennsylvania adopted a policy in 1898 of reforestation along its lines east of Pittsburgh. Joseph Beale and J. T. Rothrock were instrumental in developing the idea. The road used about 3,000,000 ties a year, at prices of fifty to seventy-five cents each. Two million seedlings were planted between 1902 and 1906, mostly black locust (*Robinia pseudoacacia*). Contrary to expectations, the trees grew slowly; they also developed poorly because they were infested with locust borers. The investment amounted to $53,000 excluding interest. In 1906 the company obtained the advice of R. C. Bryant of the Forest Service and hired a professional forester, Ernest Sterling, away from the Forest Service. Bryant believed planting would pay and advised the railroad to allot $10,000 per year for the next several years. Between 1906 and 1913 another 3,500,000 seedlings were planted, chiefly red oaks. Calculations for the second series of plantings (table 4) indicated that ties could be produced at forty-eight cents each. However, the following diagram (fig. 14) shows how the cost was affected by assumptions about the length of rotation, yield, and rate of interest. The assumed rotation of forty years and yield of four hundred ties per acre were very uncertain, and the interest rate used, 4.5 percent, was not a realistic rate of return given the high risks.

Beginning in 1909 the Pennsylvania attempted forest management as well as planting. Between 1909 and 1912 the railroad made improvement cuttings on 1,350 acres of natural second-growth hardwoods. The cuts yielded 16,000 ties and 2,700,000 board feet of lumber and left the woods "in better

Table 3. Expected returns, 1905, 1907, 1909 from catalpa plantations, Burlington, dollars per acre.

Expectations of 1905

Rotation: 20 years
Yield: 219 ties per acre plus posts
Interest rate: none accounted

Cost to plant and cultivate		15.00
Returns in 7–8 years (1914), posts at 5 cents	32.50	
Returns in 20 years (1926), ties at 50 cents	110.00	
		142.50

Net return 127.50

Expectations of 1907

Rotation: 20 years
Yield: 420 ties per acre, posts and cordwood
Interest rate: 5 percent

Cost of land, rent at $3 per acre per year	99.00	
Cost to plant and cultivate, with interest	120.00	
		219.00
Returns in 10 years (1916), with interest		
posts at 5 cents	34.00	
Returns in 20 years (1926)		
ties at 60 cents net	250.00	
posts at 5 cents	21.00	
cordwood at $1	2.00	
		307.00

Net return	88.00
Net return per year	4.40

Expectations of 1909

Rotation:	25 years	
Yield:	696 ties per acre, plus posts	
Interest rate:	5 percent	
Cost of land, rent at $3 per acre per year		75.00
Cost to plant and cultivate		47.00
Additional cultivation		61.00
Interest		134.00
		317.00
Returns in 10 years (1918)		
posts at 12 cents		78.00
interest		59.00
Returns in 25 years (1933)		
ties at 75 cents		520.00
posts at 12 cents		84.00
		741.00
Net return		424.00
Net return per year		16.92

Sources: MS, File CB&Q G Catalpa, Burlington Lines, Galesburg, Illinois: letter of John P. Brown to J. D. Besler, Oct. 13, 1905, planning a 400-acre planting on idle Burlington land on the Missouri River; report of Sept. 7, 1907, to Vice-President Daniel Willard, on actual 115-acre plantation; report of Oct. 13, 1909, on same plantation, figures adjusted to allow for losses in 1907 and replanting in 1908. By this time the Burlington was paying 68 cents per tie.

Table 4. Pennsylvania Railroad plantations, expectations, 1906.

Rotation:	40 years		
Yield:	400 ties per acre		
Interest rate:	4.5 percent		
		Dollars per acre	
Cost of land with interest		58.16	
Cost of plants and planting		58.16	
Taxes		3.21	
Management and protection		16.05	
Harvest (cutting and sawing ties)		40.00	
Hauling ties		20.00	
Total cost per acre			195.58
Total cost per tie			.48

Source: Ernest A. Sterling, "Artificial Reproduction of Forests," *Forestry Quarterly,* VI (June 1908), 211–219.

condition." On this operation the Forester, now John Foley, calculated an immediate profit of more than $13,000, and a cost of about five cents per thousand board feet for practicing forestry. Company lands under forest management were increased to a maximum of 100,000 acres, largely watershed property owned by the Pennsylvania's subsidiary water companies.[26]

The Delaware and Hudson Railroad attempted forestry, apparently under pressure from the complex interests allied with the Adirondack Park.[27] The motives were mixed. From the 1890s the Adirondack railroads had been attacked by forestry journals such as Sargent's *Garden and Forest* for fires caused by locomotive sparks. "When a railroad penetrates the recesses of a hardwood forest its destruction is absolutely certain."[28] In 1903 the D&H acquired one of the offending rail lines, an ore and iron company, which had been burning charcoal, but converted to coke, and 100,000 acres of land, mostly cutover hardwoods, adjacent to the Adirondack Park.

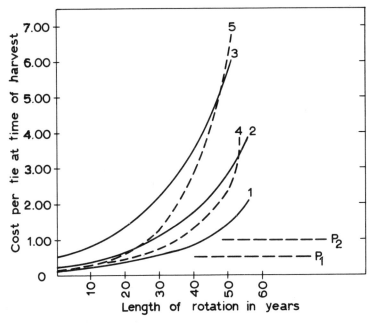

14. Interest Charges and Uncertainty of Investment in Plantations

P_1 Average price of oak tie, U.S., 1906
P_2 Price expectation of 1906 for 1926
Investment cost assumed of $50 per acre for land, plants, and labor

Curve	Rate of interest (percent)	Expected yield, ties per acre
1	5	400
2	5	200
3	5	100
4	6	400
5	8	400

The railroad immediately had the Bureau of Forestry survey the lands, then contracted to sell the remaining hardwoods for lumber and softwoods for pulp. The D&H established nurseries in 1906 and 1910 and made plantings from 1908 with the idea of providing ties.[29]

Other railroads took advantage of technical services offered by the Bureau of Forestry. Land was generally being held for nonforest purposes, and its cost did not enter into calculation of profitability of forestry. Like the Delaware and Hudson, the New York Central and Hudson River Railroad applied for surveys and working plans in 1903, probably under the pressure of agitation over forest fires in the Adirondacks. With great fanfare the Baltimore and Ohio purchased 125,000 acres near Camden-on-Gauley, West Virginia, and held a meeting of the President, L. F. Loree, and 200 officials to listen to two days of lectures on forestry. After the Bureau of Forestry developed a working plan and appraised the timber, the railroad promptly sold the land at a profit.[30] The Milwaukee (Chicago, Milwaukee and St. Paul Railway) obtained a survey "of the future supply of ties" in Wisconsin and Minnesota. The West Coast land grant railroads had their forest holdings assessed, apparently in relation to their kaleidoscopic buying and selling. The Union Pacific had its forest lands examined. The Northern Pacific, probably the largest holder of timberland in the nation, requested advice on lumber operations as early as 1898. Soon afterward, it sold off large blocks of the best timber, notably to F. E. Weyerhaeuser. Under special forest lieu selection acts (1897–1905), it also traded mediocre holdings in new Mount Rainier Park and surrounding national forest for excellent timberlands in 1898–1899. The Long Island Railroad had wastelands studied. Under Forest Service technical plans the Kirby Lumber Company produced ties in a loblolly pine tract in Texas; the tract was being held for later development of oil.

By 1915 when the above examples were studied by other railroads, it was evident that plantations did not produce direct financial returns. They were justified only on other grounds, such as windbreaks, snow fences in the prairies, beautification of station grounds, tax benefits, or the results of the research they produced. Even as demonstration plots for farmers they were not effective except in the prairies. The railroads discovered that production of commercial species takes longer than they had supposed or could afford to undertake. They found that the short-rotation species would not yield timber of quality suitable for their purposes or for other markets. They learned that risks of disease and poor form were large, particularly in plantations of a single species. Rates of return of 4 or 5 percent were not sufficient to justify plantations. It was not reasonable to expect railroad managements to pursue these projects with consistent care and regular investment over such a long period of years. The railroads were subject to fluctuating earnings and capital shortages, and they already sustained heavy burdens of capital and other fixed costs. Neglect of trees for short periods added heavily to the risk and probable losses.

By 1915 the Santa Fe had tempered its zeal for planting. No new plantings had been made for two years because of drought. "The growth of trees is too slow to make planting a practical commercial proposition . . . it will take too long under present conditions for them to attain the necessary size, hence there is no intention of continuing the planting." [31] The Delaware and Hudson continued planting, but the assumptions and objectives were modified: "The company does not consider it wise to plant trees for railroad purposes on account of the time element and possibility of using substitute materials in railroad construction." [32] Poplar was planted instead with the idea of producing pulp timber in twenty to twenty-five years and pine for general lumber in forty to fifty years. The Pennsylvania continued "manage-ment" of its forest lands, but the rationale changed: the primary use was protection of watersheds. The PRR aban-doned planting except for live hedges that would act as snow fences and landscaping to screen signs. Besler continued to indulge his whim for catalpa on the Burlington.

When the railroads began to experience rising costs of timber (1895–1907), the interpretation of the Forest Service led them to believe that the trend would continue and that the only way to avoid "famine" was to increase supply by plantings and forest protection. Major railroads undertook experiments in forestry. Although they were small-scale opera-tions, they were, nevertheless, the largest series of private forestry experiments in the United States until the late 1930s. The first results of these experiments brought disfavor to forestry as a commercial proposition.

Chapter 6

"An Unbridged Gap"

From about 1910 to 1915 the railroads became increasingly disillusioned with forestry and increasingly suspicious of the Forest Service depletion theory. Although their forestry experiments were not meeting expectations, they were finding real payoffs in a different approach to the tie question: more efficient and more limited use of timber. As railroad men analyzed their own fresh experiences, they began to revise their expectations for the future. They found foresters reluctant to face new facts. The two groups of managers no longer saw the nation's timber problem from the same point of view. In the first decade of the century the resource managers and the consumers had joined hands, but after 1910 they gradually became estranged.

Foresters must take a large share of the blame for the estrangement. The railroads had asked for advice on forestry and regarded the foresters as technical experts. Pinchot and his subordinates, in creating a profession, had encouraged their faith by emphasizing the importance of training in silviculture and by the dogmatic character of their publications. The quality of the advice given by the Forest Service, however, disappointed the railroads. They were advised to adopt practices in line with an idealized concept of "good forestry," instead of forest practices that would actually promote railroad economies.

About 1904, for example, government foresters were promoting the half-round tie and the short eight-foot tie, in order to save wood, although the railroad engineers knew they could get longer service and greater economy from heavier, longer ties of rectangular cross section. The Forest Service urged tie makers to cut trees larger than their customary standard of eleven to fourteen inches in diameter, in order to let the small ones grow for products of higher value. Tie makers resisted the idea because it put tie making into competition with those lumber products of higher value that could be cut only from larger trees. By urging that larger trees be cut to make smaller ties, the Forest Service was promoting an economic contradiction from the railroads' point of view. Railroad engineers had their way, of course, and the trend of the next fifty years was toward ties larger in all dimensions. Tie manufacturers began, consequently, to take somewhat larger trees on the average and left the eleven- and twelve-inch trees. In other words, the consumer rejected the foresters' advice and discovered a policy that was more efficient for him and ultimately more effective as a conservation measure.

The Forest Service also "failed" the railroads by advising them to plant fast-growing species. Forest Service publications reproduced success stories based on these species.[1] The railroads were obliged to accept Forest Service estimates of growth and survival of trees as long as they had no contradictory evidence, but, as they accumulated experience to the contrary, they abandoned the guidance of the Forest Service.

In the Forest Service administration, furthermore, the left hand seemed not to know what the right hand was doing. A few engineers in the products branch of the Forest Service were working closely with railroad managers on techniques for wood preservation. By 1906 railroad managers began to realize that wood preservation would cut their needs for ties, that utilization of easily treated species such as the red oaks and pines would increase the supply, and that substitution of concrete or steel for wood in bridges and buildings would reduce demand further. While Forest Service product engineers were predicting, measuring, and encouraging these changes, Forest Service silviculturists were ignoring them. The silviculturists continued through World War I to predict rising prices for wood, critical shortages, and a painful "wood famine." They continued to agitate for large investments in plantations and forest holding as profitable and patriotic ventures.

As a consequence, from about 1910 railroad men became wary of the economic and silvicultural advice of the Forest Service. Railway engineers maintained a formal liaison with conservation groups without playing a vital role.[2] Their concern with growing wood as the ultimate solution to the tie question gave way to the conviction that the solution to the conservation issue lay in reducing the consumption of wood. A Pennsylvania Railroad man explained this in 1910. "So far, much less emphasis has been placed on the equally important question of reducing the consumption of forest products. It is very well to make any area produce two sticks of timber where before there was but one; still, it is just as good lumber economy to double the life of the first stick, and there is the added advantage of an immense saving to the consumer."[3]

The brief period of most intense interest by railway managements in forest planting coincided with rapid professionalization and specialization among both railway engineers and foresters. A tiny hybrid class developed of "railroad foresters" who were trained in the Forest Service and hired by the railroads. Among the most perceptive and influential were Ernest Sterling and Hermann von Schrenk. They participated in the professional societies of both foresters and railway engineers over several decades, and these two men personify changing views of the tie question among railroad men between 1907 or 1908 and World War I.

In 1907 Sterling became forester of the Pennsylvania Railroad. This was the first appointment of a "technically trained forester" by a railroad and was hailed by professional foresters and forestry magazines as a great step forward. The Pennsylvania Railroad has continued to the present to employ foresters as supervisors of ties and timber. The forester also oversees wood preservation. All have been active in such organizations as American Wood Preservers' Association (AWPA), AREA, and the Society of American Foresters (SAF). Sterling took over the black locust plantations and diversified them with species that were slower growing. Red oak, for example, was adapted to the sites and suitable for use as treated ties. He continued to urge artificial reproduction, that is, plantation forestry. He considered it profitable where the railroad utilized wastelands "which they must hold in any event." [4]

During the period 1909–1911 Sterling was the most influential spokesman of railroad forestry. He was, however, a hardheaded skeptic. "We like to consider it [railroad forestry] a necessity, but if it were it would be more generally practiced. The truth is that there is an unbridged gap between the theory and the sentiment on the subject and the hard economics of railroad management." [5] As a forester, he preached depletion to the railroads, but, as a railroad man, he demanded economic information from the foresters: "The things about forestry which the railroads desire to know, the Government has not been prepared to tell them . . . In order to get started, the railroads need help in the form of conclusive data which will show that forestry will fit in with their present commercial activities."[6] He especially objected to Forest Service propaganda work because it stubbornly ignored facts of interest to the railroads. For example, government forestry publications disregarded farmers' woodlots in estimating timber supplies. "The tie supply in the East is drawn largely from small woodlots, and in many regions the output is as great now as it was twenty years ago. Knowing this, railroad managers are in doubt whether to be alarmed over the general statements that the timber supply will be gone in twenty or thirty years . . . To ignore the woodlots in estimating the nation's timber supply not only introduces an error into the computations but reduces confidence."[7]

In 1909 the Pennsylvania began treating crossties, and Sterling took a large part in wood-preserving research. He considered wood preservation an integral part, but not a complete plan, for railroad forestry. He ceased to advocate plantings except on small wastelands and argued that the way to solve the supply problem was to reserve timberlands and manage them so that they would produce indefinitely. "My feeling about forest planting is that it is a mighty good thing to do when a railroad has waste land . . . but it will not solve the tie supply problem. If the railroads want any assurance of getting good timber 15 or 20 years hence, there is only one way, to buy mature timberland in fee . . . We will be not only helping ourselves as individuals and corporations, but the nation as well."[8]

Sterling was elected President of the American Wood Preservers' Association in 1912. He still believed that a crisis would be reached that would "affect national prosperity to such an extent as to force a solution of our timber supply problem." [9] He observed the coincidence between early work on wood preservation around 1865 and the early anticipation of a timber shortage. "They both failed of general acceptance at the time because of the vast quantities of cheap timber available." But by this time he recommended that forest management should be undertaken not locally on each rail line, but in the South where the growing conditions were most favorable, with fast-growing native stands such as loblolly pine. He also recommended that wood-preserving companies, rather than railroads, undertake forest management. "A treating plant should have back of it a definite source of timber supply." [10]

The Pennsylvania's experience on thirty thousand acres of mature timber reflected Sterling's ideas. Logging was carried out which left the properties "in a much more productive state than before." He advised management, treating, and control of forest fires in the interest of the railroads. "The railroads are not in the treating business for the purpose of saving the forests, but to save money." [11]

By 1915, when Sterling became one of the directors of the American Forestry Association, he had moved still further from his original ideas. "The phantom of timber famine has never been very real, and its use as a bugaboo or club has been a boomerang." [12] Sterling had steadily pursued the idea that forest conservation was "a purely economic problem." "Conservation that does not pay will not conserve. The country needs economic, not sentimental, forest conservation." [13] But this approach led him to a position at odds with traditional forestry. He found that the conservation agitation of the past decade had "put the possibilities of conservation farther away than ever" by encouraging the "unjustified use of substitutes" and by inspiring speculative buying of timber.

The ownership of mature reserve timber was now threatening the solvency of timberland owners, and capital could not be invested in forest production from the seedling or volunteer young growth stage. The reduced demand for timber kept prices low and thus made conservative forestry unprofitable.

Hermann von Schrenk was at once a scientist trained as a plant pathologist, an engineer, and an economist. He was at various times railroad consultant, government forester, educator, and wood preserver, and he looked at problems from all points of view. Like Sterling, he regarded the basic problem as economic, that is, a matter of costs. This allowed him to analyze effectively the relevance of European experience to the American problem. He was never committed to any method or doctrine other than economy. In 1902, when he was associated with the Bureau of Forestry and the Bureau of Plant Industry, von Schrenk accepted the idea of depletion and the expectation that in the future the rapid-growth species such as catalpa and eucalyptus would be planted to produce ties. He was, however, already more interested in the large supply of "inferior" timbers that could be used with chemical treatment.

> Figures as to the actual amount of timber cut are difficult to obtain, and after all they give the average reader very little intelligent information . . . Although it is not probable that we are to face a timber famine in the near future, it can hardly be denied that removal . . . cannot fail to make a deep impression on the forest resources . . .

> Could the [supply] be drawn on rationally, it would tend to establish an equilibrium, which would react favorably on the lumber industry, and at the same time tend to save some of those timbers more valuable for the higher kinds of structural requirements.

By increasing the length of service of timber, we not only make it cheaper, but we use less of it.[14]

In 1903 he refused to predict a timber famine, but he believed there would be a "state of uncertainty and worry, possibly rising prices."[15] He recommended forest management with selective lumbering for sizes of highest value "when we know the rate at which trees grow," planting fast-growing species on wastelands, and preservation and seasoning. Management of fast-growing species of timber would be integrated with timber preservation.

In 1907 von Schrenk talked depletion, but he was consciously using it as a weapon toward business economy in consumption first and in forestry second. He had separated from the Bureau of Forestry. As a consultant on wood preserving to numerous railroads, he was skeptical of railroad forestry experiments and favored channeling investment into wood preservation and mechanical protection of ties. He argued that more could be accomplished by economical use of timber than by scientific forestry "because it affects the individual user of wood more directly."

It behooves every person who uses wood to any extent to consider the matter of present and future supply . . . for two reasons. The first one, a personal one: because it will lead him, as I hope to show you, toward practices of economy in the use of his material. The second, a consideration for himself in the future, as well as a consideration for future generations.

I am a firm believer, however, that the best way to insure a consideration for the future is to demonstrate clearly the possibility from a financial standpoint of adopting such measures for our present benefit as will at the same time work in the interests of the coming generations.[16]

Von Schrenk and Sterling emphasized the necessity for a coincidence of sentimental and commercial interests if conservation was to occur. The forestry endorsed by the sentimental interests was, however, becoming less appealing to commercial consumers as they developed their new practices of economy in the use of material.

Parallel with their campaign to protect the supply of timber, the railroads conducted a campaign to cut back their use of timber. They adopted much of the technology that had been created over the last twenty years. Enthusiasm for various panaceas reached a peak about 1904, when the Universal Exposition was held at St. Louis. All aspects of the "tie question" were exhibited there, as were all proposed solutions. There were concrete ties, rolled steel ties from Prussia, cast-iron pot sleepers, quebracho wood from Argentina, eucalyptus ties from Australia, creosoted and zinc-tannin treated ties. General William J. Palmer's Arboriculture Society exhibited catalpa passenger car furnishings. The Bureau of Forestry featured woodlot plantations of the "tie species," novel ways of fastening the rail to the tie, and an operating wood-preserving pilot plant, timber-testing station, and laboratory. The sixteen acres of railway exhibits included substitutes for wood in other uses, such as all-steel freight cars, corrugated steel doors, and a model of a harbor terminal built without wood. Cement manufacturers performed physical tests while the Geological Survey tested other structural materials, cement and clay.[17] It was not yet apparent even to the most competent observers what impact the various devices would have on railway economy. For example, the editors of the *Railway and Engineering Review* reported that there had been no "radical inventions" since the World's Columbian Exposition at Chicago in 1893.

By 1908 or 1910, however, certain techniques began to benefit the large railroads that pioneered them, and by 1915 the most promising solutions were sifted out. The most important—the "radical invention"—was the adoption of wood preserving. With it were associated many other changes in practice, substitution of new species and materials, and the more efficient allocation of timbers to various uses.

Wood Preserving

Within fifteen years an industry of the scale now observed was created. Between 80 and 95 percent of the output went to railroad consumers, and many plants were built with railroad capital. Where there were 14 plants in 1900, there were over 70, including much larger ones, in 1907, and 102 in 1915. Graphs (figs. 16 and 17) and a map (fig. 15) show the extraordinary expansion of the industry in terms of the number of treating plants, volume of materials consumed, and the quantities of ties and other timber treated. The proportion of ties treated increased from less than 5 percent to about 30 percent of all ties purchased.

Rapid change took place initially on large railroads. In 1899 the Burlington, for example, built its first treating plant at Edgemont, South Dakota, and put a water chemist from its testing laboratory in charge. By 1910 the railroad was treating all crossties in two plants [18] and was beginning to treat a wider variety of bridge and car materials. The 1908 standards of treatment were practiced until about 1930.

The expansion in the quantity of creosote used was more rapid than the expansion of the quantity of wood treated. This indicates an important qualitative change. The railroads that treated wood before 1903 were using mainly zinc chloride, an inexpensive and only moderately efficient process. In 1907 over half the ties treated were still injected with zinc chloride; by 1911 the figure was only 29 percent. Railroads began to use either creosote alone or creosote as a supplement to zinc

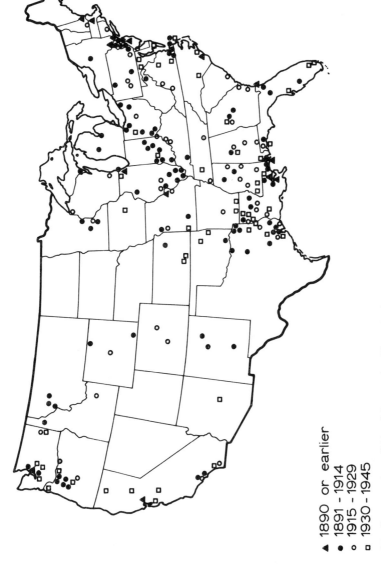

▲ 1890 or earlier
● 1891 - 1914
○ 1915 - 1929
□ 1930 - 1945

15. Construction of Wood-Preserving Plants in the U.S.

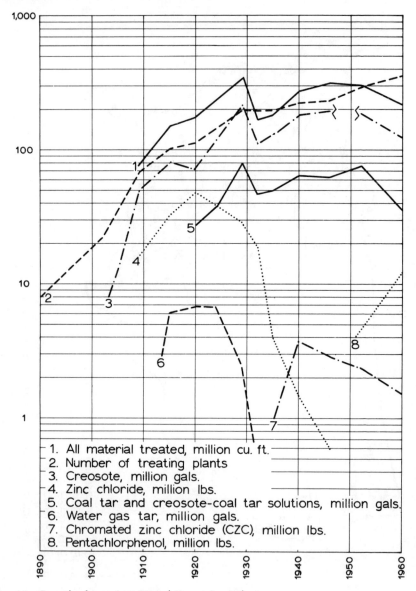

1. All material treated, million cu. ft.
2. Number of treating plants
3. Creosote, million gals.
4. Zinc chloride, million lbs.
5. Coal tar and creosote-coal tar solutions, million gals.
6. Water gas tar, million gals.
7. Chromated zinc chloride (CZC), million lbs.
8. Pentachlorphenol, million lbs.

16. Growth of American Wood-Preserving Industry

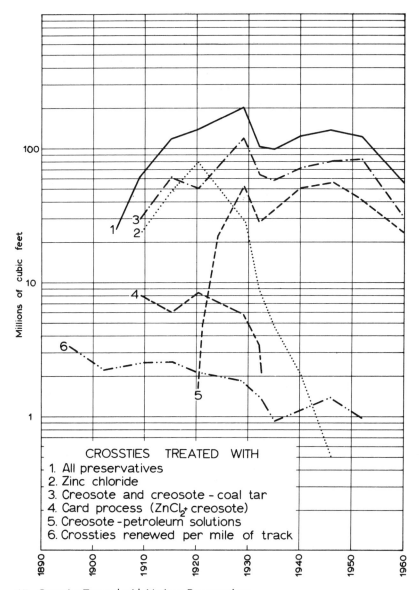

CROSSTIES TREATED WITH
1. All preservatives
2. Zinc chloride
3. Creosote and creosote - coal tar
4. Card process (ZnCl$_2$+ creosote)
5. Creosote - petroleum solutions
6. Crossties renewed per mile of track

17. Crossties Treated with Various Preservatives

chloride. Users of creosote increased the amount of creosote they injected per cubic foot of wood.[19] The use of more creosote was encouraged by its falling price. Creosote is derived from coal tar, a by-product of steel manufacture, and growth and technical changes in the steel industry had a strong, positive effect on the supply of creosote to the market. All these changes meant larger investment in treatment and longer service life for ties.

A modest wood-preserving plant cost forty thousand to fifty thousand dollars, a small amount of capital in proportion to the eventual annual savings. The value of treated material handled each year was five to ten times the capital cost of the plant. Operating costs for the first ten years represented a larger investment before returns would begin, unless cheaper "inferior" woods could be substituted. The incentive to treat wood depended on the cost of treatment, the cost of the timber, and the expected life of the treated product. Neither the life of the various species with various treatments nor the minimum quantities of preservative necessary to obtain desired service life were known. The cost of the chemical preservatives represented about two-thirds of the cost of treatment, as practiced on the Burlington.

By 1910 calculations of annual cost made treated ties cheaper than untreated ones on an increasing number of railroads. Expectations of rising tie prices created a sense of alarm, especially among railroads that imported ties from other regions. This encouraged treatment.

However, fluctuations of the business cycle retarded the adoption of wood preservation and orderly purchasing practices. "Unfortunately the policy of many roads is to refuse to consider the matter [wood preservation] when the price of ties is weak, because of the temporary cheapening of the supply; and to refuse to embark in it when the price of ties is high, because then it is impossible to contract for a supply of ties except at the higher prices."[20] The Interstate Commerce Commission adopted a new accounting system in 1908 (revised in 1914) that required railroads to charge treated ties to operating expenses, even where they were inserted to replace untreated ties of lesser value. Longer lasting rails and fastenings were "betterments," and the difference between the cost of the old and the new heavier rail or plates was accounted a capital investment. This accounting method discriminated against treated ties.

The new discoveries arising from research made wood preserving cheaper or extended the life expectancy of the treated tie and reduced the cost of preserving calculated on an annual basis. For example, one reason for the efficiency of creosote as a preservative was attributed to its oily character, which prevented moisture from penetrating the timber. The other principal reason, understood earlier, was, of course, the toxicity of creosote to fungi and marine worms. Understanding the role of creosote as a moisture inhibitor made possible the development of cheaper solutions of creosote in coal tar and petroleum. They were widely adopted after 1920 (see fig. 12).

Work by H. D. Tiemann at the Forest Products Laboratory clarified the relationship of wood structure to ease of treatment, rate of seasoning, and penetrability of wood to various depths. His work established a theoretical basis for seasoning experiments and the sorting of species for treatment. Empirical tests at the same time provided the first useful information on treatment of the "mixed hardwoods"—hardwoods such as hickory and oak, or maple, birch, and beech, usually found growing together in mixed stands.

Mechanical tests of timber demonstrated the importance of reducing temperatures of treatment. The presence of steam injured the wood and reduced its strength. Railroads began to restrict steaming and treatment temperatures. For the same reasons, they reduced the strength of the zinc chloride solutions they used from 4 or 5 percent to 2 or 2.5 percent.

Changes Associated with Wood Preserving

Many important changes in the use of wood were closely related to progress in its preservation. New species were accepted, and new methods were adopted for manufacturing, handling, sorting, seasoning, and distributing ties (see fig. 18).

Wood preservation enlarged the supply of timbers suitable for crossties. The "inferior species," that is, the cheaper kinds of wood that if untreated decayed rapidly, were treated and substituted for the relatively durable white oak. The red oaks [21] were abundant in the same regions as the white oaks, and their use increased. Treated hemlock and tamarack entered production in large volumes in the states bordering on the Great Lakes, nearly five million ties in 1905. The use of cedar began to decline, displaced by treated timbers. Durable foreign woods from Japan, Hawaii, and Australia were tested and found more expensive than the treated domestic "inferior species."

Treatment made advantageous a rather elaborate allocation of the several species to various conditions of service. About 1908–1910 the Santa Fe, Pennsylvania, Northern Pacific, and Burlington, among others, established definite systems of geographical distribution in track for ties of several species and treatments. Hardwood ties were reserved for curves and grades, softwood ties for tangent track. The untreated white oak was reserved for steep grades, sharp curves, and heavy traffic zones where it would wear out before decay destroyed it.[22] The treated species, if given such punishment, would have worn out before their added life could be realized because many of the new timbers were softer. The cellular structures

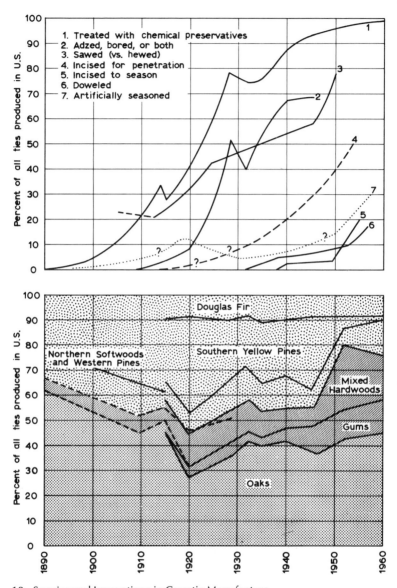

18. Species and Innovations in Crosstie Manufacture

that made them absorb preservatives readily also gave them less desirable mechanical properties. Ties treated with zinc chloride were placed in arid districts, while those treated with creosote or zinc chloride and creosote were reserved for the wet areas. The same principle of careful allocation was also applied to larger timber structures. The soft shortleaf and loblolly pines were utilized for temporary structures (false-work), and the denser, harder, and stronger pieces and long-leaf pine were treated and reserved for permanent structures.

Ties manufactured by sawing became acceptable to the railroads during this period. The hewed tie had the advantage, appreciated early, of containing more wood; its irregularities meant that for a stated size and price it was always over-size. Presumably this added strength to the track. Conditions after 1900 revealed the advantages of sawed ties. Because they were uniform and were smaller on the average, they weighed less and therefore saved freight. The uniform volume of sawed ties permitted more uniform absorption during pressure treatment. In the track, uniformity of sawed ties assured uniform bearing and made adzing (planing) unnecessary. Uniform bearing meant better quality track and less wear on individual ties.

From the point of view of the tie maker, sawing ties produced marketable by-products called tie siding—boards and flooring—instead of waste chips. The transition to manufacture by sawing integrated tie production into the larger markets for lumber. All sizes of trees could be sawed into ties and tie siding, whereas economical hewing of ties was a specialized operation limited to trees of about eleven to fifteen inches in diameter. New sources of power were harnessed that made small "peckerwood" sawmills available to the farmer-operator. The small mills were portable, that is, they could be dismantled, moved, and reassembled in a few hours or a day. They were, therefore, economical for working small lots of timber characteristic of the tie industry in the Midwest and South and were ideal for rugged country in the Appalachians and Rockies, where it was not practicable to haul logs to large mills.

As a result of changes in the demand for sawed ties and tie siding, and the availability of portable sawmills, production of sawed ties reached 15 percent of all ties made in 1909 and 25 percent by 1915 and developed rapidly after that (see fig. 18 above). The results were not immediately apparent, but, eventually, diversification and mechanization of the producer's operation permitted economies that increased supply.

By 1912 air seasoning was practiced for the majority of ties treated. The importance of seasoning ties to achieve effective treatment was recognized in Octave Chanute's report to the American Society of Civil Engineers (1885) and publications of the Division of Forestry (1890s). Steaming was discouraged and gradually abandoned except for Douglas fir. For car lumber drying in kilns came into use. The Norfolk and Western Railway built the first dry kiln on Tiemann's plan of humidity control. But for timbers of lower value, such as crossties, air seasoning was the most economical method. Experimentation determined the proper length of time to season various species; the species were grouped for treatment according to the moisture content. Seasoning before shipment produced significant savings on freight. For example, in 1902–1903 the Burlington's cooperative experiments with von Schrenk in seasoning lodgepole pine in Wyoming demonstrated that 39 percent of the weight of ties was lost by open-air drying.

The question of seasonal restrictions on cutting was settled. The old rule of thumb requiring winter cut of ties had been useful not because of "rising sap," but because of the summer weather conducive to fungous growth. Once clearly understood, the seasonal handicap could be overcome by careful handling and seasoning. Decay could be prevented even in the summer months—a major accomplishment of the period 1902–1915. Ties were peeled and piled openly to permit ventilation, instead of being left scattered on the damp fungus-infested ground; they were piled on treated blocks instead of on infected ties; and they were taken out of the woods promptly to supervised seasoning yards.

Standardizing antiseptic practices in tie production and handling was more difficult than innovations such as wood preserving. A large number of people, widely dispersed and, on the whole, uneducated and fiercely independent, had to be convinced. The railroad inspectors and purchasing agents achieved this through constant agitation and the use of incentive cash payments for peeling and piling ties. They decided not to accept ties cut over a month before delivery. Where one railroad was the sole buyer in a territory, it was reasonably easy to enforce specifications of this kind, but where railroads competed for ties, cyclical buying and the failure to agree on a standard undermined quality.

The railroads also had to educate their own laborers to handle treated products. Special tools, tie tongs, were issued. Handling ties with a pick was forbidden. Adzing (planing the surface under the rail or tie plate) was also discouraged because it left wounds that exposed untreated wood to dampness and contamination.

Use of a wider variety of species and the requirements of uniform seasoning and treatment made it necessary to group species. By 1910 the Burlington was receiving ties by barge at Joppa, Illinois. They were inspected, paid for, then sorted and loaded into separate cars of hardwoods and softwoods. When they arrived at the Galesburg treating plant, they were unloaded and piled in a "hard yard" and a "soft yard" for seasoning. Once seasoned, they were re-sorted into three treating classes (the Burlington found it cheaper to re-sort the ties than to enforce sorting by the producer). At their Sheridan plant the problem was simpler, since Douglas fir was received separately from a different region, seasoned separately, and treated apart from the other western softwoods, lodgepole and bull pine. The Santa Fe, like the Burlington, did its own sorting at the treating plant and handled few species. The difficult problems arose in the region of mixed hardwood forests and were eventually thrust back on the producers. The New York Central, for example, required contractors or producers to group and load five classes of hardwoods separately. Enforcement cost about one cent per tie for inspection.

Mechanical protection of ties was associated with treatment. Railroads that invested in treated ties sought to protect that investment. When the Tie Committee of the AREA analyzed the causes of tie failure in 1908, they found that decay was still the first cause, but began to pay more attention to the effects of mechanical stresses. Tie plates and new fastenings were designed to protect ties, and by 1901 tie plates were standard on eighteen railroads. A report of 1912 urged adoption of smooth-bottomed plates that would not injure the wood fibers the way the older lug plates did. About 1909 most railroads expressed interest in the screw spike fastening.

Heavier and more scientific track construction with stiffer rail, wider rail base, and deeper and better ballast contributed to longer tie life. Theoretical work on track stresses led to design of longer lasting rail and permitted the use of heavier equipment and faster trains. In a 1907 engineering bulletin, O. E. Selby argued that not a single detail of track superstructure bore the marks of engineering design. He attempted to apply bridge design theory to track. Girders, piers, footings, and foundations of bridges were compared, respectively, to the rails, ties, ballast, and subgrade of track. His calculations showed that all stresses in track were far greater than the safety rules for bridge design permitted. The margin of safety for stresses on ties was especially small.

Selby recommended heavier rail, 100 to 115 pounds per yard, tie plates of at least 50 square inches in area, ties 8 feet 6 inches long and of 7 inch by 9 inch cross section, and ballast of the best quality, 18 inches deep. His analysis of the trade-off among rail weight, tie size, depth of ballast, and spacing of ties made it possible to consider the tie as an engineered object.[23] The Tie Committee found that year that thirty out of fifty-one railroads were using smaller ties than recommended, 6 inches by 8 inches by 8 feet. The Pennsylvania Railroad calculated that where plates were not used the average load on the tie under the rail was between 800 and 900 pounds per square inch, close to the normal average strength of oak and yellow pine. This explained why rails often cut deep into the ties and shortened their life. By using tie plates, which distributed the load to a larger area of the tie, the maximum pressure was reduced to about 525 pounds per square inch.[24] Engineering studies of track structure developed rapidly in the next few years. The AREA created a special committee on impact tests and raised a fund of ten thousand dollars to combine theoretical work with large-scale empirical tests. E. E. Stetson, for example, computed stresses produced in track by locomotives rounding curves at various speeds.

Substitution of Materials

As the fear of depletion reached its crisis about 1908, there was more and more discussion of substitution. The technical possibilities were developed further, and flexibility in the use of materials was achieved. By 1915, however, the pattern of substitution of materials in railway practice was quite different from what had been predicted.

Between 1900 and 1915 the committees of the large engineering societies did more work on standards and specifications for materials than on any other subject. (After World I, signaling, electrical, and labor problems generated more intense interest.) The ASCE, the AREA, and the ASTM did important work on cement, steel, and reinforced concrete. They also paid more attention to wood than at any time before or since. The railway engineers gave close attention to design of concrete, steel, and reinforced concrete crossties.[25] In 1903–1904 their bridge committees were pessimistic about the future of the wood bridge. Wood bridges were classified as temporary (the wood bridge committee of the Railway Engineering Association was separated from steel and masonry design), and it was believed that steel, concrete, earthwork, and stone structures would soon replace wood structures. The concern of these bridge engineers was based on changing cost ratios and the conviction that depletion was the cause of the cost changes and would continue indefinitely.

Both committees studied timber and concrete trestle design with a conservation bias in favor of concrete. "We err in the installation of wood when concrete will answer."[26] The Burlington constructed the first precast concrete trestles in 1906 and between 1909 and 1911 built twenty thousand linear feet of reinforced concrete trestle of pile bent design, that is, patterned after the older wood trestles.

International railway congresses held every few years stimulated interest in substitution. These congresses gave the prestige of "worldwide trends" to local concerns about expected wood shortages. They introduced into the United States the practices common on European railways and featured extensively the German controversy over steel ties and French use of screw spikes and plates that reinforced rail joints and stiffened track.

The federal government built a laboratory costing $140,000 for the Bureau of Standards and expanded its work rapidly between 1901 and 1915. Together with the Geological Survey, responsible for inventorying mineral resources including building materials, the Bureau of Standards carried out a special program of research on structural materials. Over ten years about a million dollars were spent. The work was justified on the grounds of fire safety, government economy in construction and purchasing, and public concern about the future supplies of coal and timber. "The Forest Service estimates that, at the present rate of consumption, renewals of growth now being taken into account, the timber supply will be exhausted within the next quarter of a century. It is desirable, therefore, that all information possible be gained regarding the most suitable substitutes for wood for building and engineering construction." [27] Testing laboratories were built at the St. Louis Exposition, then transferred elsewhere, and results on cements and clay products effectively reduced the "uncertainty as to how most of these materials can be used efficiently in relation to one another because of the lack of authentic data as to their strength, elasticity, permeability, and other properties, also as to their behavior under high temperatures . . ." [28]

As a result of greater understanding of the properties of materials, iron, steel, and concrete were substituted in some railroad uses but not others. There was a rapid shift between 1900 and 1914 from all-wood to all-metal passenger cars and freight cars with metal frames and wood bodies. The change was associated with safety campaigns and high costs of car repairs. Production of fence posts shifted in large part from wood to concrete and metal. In bridge timber there was some substitution of steel trusses and concrete pile trestle. Most wood bridges and trestles after 1910 were renewed with standard ballast deck trestles of treated wood. This type of trestle, first standardized on the prairie and southern railroads, proved competitive in service life and annual cost with the so-called "permanent structures." A ballast deck trestle has a standard track laid in ballast on top of a wood deck. The ballast fireproofs the bridge against locomotive cinders. Standard track made it possible to use regular track labor for maintenance instead of expensive bridge repair gangs required on the older "open deck" bridges. Substitution of steel and concrete for ties and telegraph poles was strictly experimental.[29]

The Adjustment Mechanism

The substitution of steel and concrete occurred in those uses in which wood preservation was not applied. Untreated wood was displaced by treated wood of new species and by concrete and steel. Substitution and wood preservation can be seen as complementary techniques for solving the same problem. Or, wood preservation may be regarded as a special case of substitution.

In the same way, grading of materials is a special case of substitution. Classes are created with a limited range of variation of the material in each class. For a particular purpose one grade is substituted for a material of greater variability, and the specific properties desired may be obtained with the greatest economy. "The value of a specification or grading rule depends largely upon its reliability in excluding material which is deemed undesirable and in admitting material adapted to the needs of the purchaser."[30]

Timber in railroad uses was not graded in a standard manner before 1900. The progress of grading in the several categories of railroad material was very uneven. Grading rules were achieved first in car lumber and in structural timber between 1900 and 1914; no real progress was made toward a standard specification for crossties until after World War I.[31] The sequence shows that grading was achieved first in the markets for materials of highest value, limited supply, and long hauls, that is, in the markets that were geographically large and diverse. Grading lagged in the products of local markets. Grading or substitution of specified average qualities of wood occurred in the uses where concrete and steel were also being substituted (cars and bridges) and where engineering research defined the desirable properties. Substitution in the crosstie market took the form of species substitution already described.

As it became economical to treat wood and eliminate the question of natural resistance to decay, engineers paid more attention to other properties of the material. For ties, elasticity and resistance to corrosion were desirable. In bridges, rapid repair was important, as were specific strength properties. Certain classes of wood had those advantages. For car frames the demand for rigidity favored the choice of steel. As the relative prices of materials varied over the years, it was gradually recognized that no material was inherently ideal for a certain purpose. It was or was not desirable for that use under a given set of economic conditions and a given technology. The technology was influenced by expectations of economic change. Erroneous expectations created a bias in the technology immediately available, but continually changing expectations and conditions produced greater understanding of alternatives, which gave greater flexibility or elasticity in the use of resources.

As the railway engineers developed materials technology and acquired that flexibility, their concern with supply waned. The railroads were committed to commercialism. They joined hands with sentimentalism in forestry only briefly. When World War I broke out, it was not yet clear which view would prevail in public forest policy.

"Use Alone Can Create Value"

The dislocations of World War I diverted attention from pre-war problems and revealed new bottlenecks in the growth of the economic system. By 1922 most shortages were disappearing (housing was an exception), but the experience had generated a strong demand for cooperation between government and business to increase the overall efficiency and flexibility of the economy. One effect was the reorientation of the American forest conservation movement about 1925 toward a new emphasis on utilization—the more efficient use of a resource. The railroads had already been moving in this direction before the war, but a new concern with labor costs added incentive to certain lines of utilization research.

Railroad Utilization of Wood

It first became clear in the 1920s, after the wartime shortages had disappeared, that the railroads as a group were definitely cutting back their consumption of timber in all uses. New track construction had become practically negligible, and by 1910 or 1915 it was apparent from the few large systems that had pioneered in wood preserving that the rate of replacement of timber could also be reduced. But there was a lag in the pay-offs. The Burlington, for example, began treating all ties in 1908, and its spending on ties declined during the 1920s (see fig. 20). Ties treated after 1910 probably had an average life of fifteen to twenty years, and therefore railroads could get a maximum payoff from the seventh or eighth year after adopting treatment to about the fifteenth year—after most of the un-treated ties had been replaced, but before most of the treated ones needed replacement. The average consumption of ties by all railroads began falling about 1908 and continued to decline throughout the 1920s.

The decade after the war was one of great innovation in maintenance of way. Three major sources of innovation are described here; in practice all were related.

The disruption of World War I was a significant factor in the innovation process on the railroads. When the U.S. entered the war in 1917, an unprecedented transport crisis developed. Because shipping was heavily weighted in one direction, from west to east, car shortages were severe, and normal market-ing patterns were disrupted. Inflation was general, but labor costs rose more than the general price level, and railroad wages, which had lagged behind other industrial wages before the war, became the object of violent controversy. A frus-trated railroad manager described the crisis as "the greatest labor demoralization the world has ever known." [1] To cope with the car shortage and labor conflict, the federal govern-ment temporarily nationalized the railroads and intervened in the railway supply industries. The U.S. Railroad Adminis-tration raised wages, reduced working hours, and reorganized railroad purchasing. Each of these actions evoked two simultaneous responses from railroad men: loud protests and adaptive innovations.

When the Railroad Administration temporarily unified purchasing of all railroads, it completely remodeled the market for railroad timber, with long-term consequences. A uniform specification and standard contract form were established for crossties, through the work of John Foley, forester for the Pennsylvania Railroad. Railroads were required to accept ties purchased and inspected by other lines. Consequently, they had to adjust their differences in standards of purchase and inspection. This process was similar to what took place when lines were consolidated, as the example of the Burlington, described in Chapter 4, shows. But the purpose of the Railroad Administration in 1918 was primarily to minimize hauling.

In spite of their strong criticism of the Forest Products Section of the Railroad Administration,[2] producers and railroads both recognized the standard specification as progressive and took steps to improve and enforce it after the railways were returned to private management in 1920. In 1922 about 75 percent of railroads were using it voluntarily. This was one example of how disruption of tradition permitted discoveries of new economies. An important tie producer put it this way late in 1918:

> The method of handling the tie production has been turned upside down in the last year. The way cross ties have been gotten out, delivered, inspected and transferred from roads that had a surplus, to the roads that had none, has all been changed, and in the new order of things, we are discovering economies that we did not suspect.

> We may go back to the same kind of a system that we had before, but we are going to consider very carefully the good things that have been developed, by having to stop

the normal natural course of our regular business. It was a business that had been developed through many years' experience and in stopping that regular channel and having to operate in another way, we have discovered good things and we want to keep them.[3]

Similar discoveries were made by railroad bridge engineers, who were told by management to maintain bridges "without any piling and stringers and without any labor"! Under pressure, they revised their standards for renewal and replacement of materials, and they found they could save money.

The effort to avoid crosshauling railway timber also forced many lines to try Douglas fir and other western species. A new technique of perforating or incising Douglas fir ties, first introduced in 1913, spread rapidly as railroads began to purchase these ties. Incising allowed preservatives to penetrate the wood more deeply and also seemed to reduce checking (the opening of fine cracks in the timber during seasoning). New specifications were written for grading Douglas fir, which had a range of variation as wide as all the southern yellow pines combined. There was continual feedback between the demand for the western species and research on the properties and treatment of those species. A crisis or a squeeze prompted discoveries, and the discoveries were found economical. From about 1924 railway revenues began to suffer from competition of motor trucking, and the squeeze of lower revenues and higher wages continued to force railroads to seek economies in all departments.

A second source of progress and new efficiency in maintenance of way was the continuing process of perfecting and spreading the techniques that had been successfully pioneered before the war. Maintenance practices that had proved economical on a few large systems before the war were widely adopted afterward, and large investments were made in track and structures during the 1920s. Most important was the progress of wood preserving. From 1920 to 1928 the proportion of crossties treated rose from 41 to 76 percent of all ties purchased. One factor in the rapid spread of crosstie treatment was a reduction of risk. Management's estimate of the risk involved in any technical change appears to be a strong factor in its decisions. By this time the costs of wood preserving were well known. Precise estimates of future average life of ties treated in various ways were controversial, but some processes were known to be effective within definite limits. The innovators of the 1920s did not take the same risks as the pioneers of the 1890s or even the early 1900s. This applies to the adoption of wood preserving, and to the important progress in standardization, and to enforcement of specifications. All these innovations were of low risk, although they required strong leadership to make administrative and organizational changes.

More experience with wood preserving made it possible to refine techniques, measure results more accurately, estimate them sooner (after fewer years of service testing), and adapt methods to a wider variety of species. Wider experimentation was encouraged by the economic and bureaucratic pressure for substitution of species. Before the war railroads had treated the red oak group, but continued to use white oaks untreated. Many large railroads found it profitable in the 1920s to treat white oak ties as well. Experience with seasoning of various species allowed more effective treatment of the "mixed hardwoods," such as maple, birch, and beech.

Wood preservers changed their preferences for preservatives. The English creosote supply was cut off during the war, and the price rose. Some railroads returned to the use of zinc chloride, but only temporarily because it did not do the same job.[4] In the longer view, price changes hastened the adoption of creosote-petroleum solutions (often 50–50 by volume). Petroleum was much cheaper than creosote and seemed to reduce checking in the ties. The first adoption of this preservative as a railroad standard was in 1920; by 1927 fifteen railroads were using it, accounting for about 20 percent of all ties treated (see fig. 16).

As treatment of ties was extended, the practice of adzing and boring ties before treatment also became general. Because preservative penetrates only a half inch or so into the sapwood, it is essential to eliminate the need to bore spike holes or plane the surface of an already treated tie. When ties are bored before treatment, better penetration of the preservative is also secured in the critical spike region where moisture and abrasion are severe and decay often begins. In the same way, the practice of preframing (prefabricating) bridge timbers was introduced, so that the railroad would get the maximum return from its investment in preservative treatment.

The railroads insisted increasingly that ties be delivered already peeled (stripped of bark) and sorted by grades and species convenient for treatment. Sawing became the dominant method of crosstie manufacture. From 1913 to 1936 the production of sawed ties went from 21 to more than 50 percent of all ties. Expansion of production in the Northwest explained part of the trend, since ties from the West Coast were produced from large timber in large, diversified sawmills. Elsewhere, improved markets for the by-products of crosstie manufacture (dimension lumber, flooring) created further incentive to sawing. But the railroads' gradual preference for sawed ties resulted mainly from progressive treatment: the wood preserver could get more uniform and more effective treatment by using only the more uniform sawed ties.

Investment in treatment also engendered further investment in mechanical protection of ties, so that treatment would pay off in maximum service life. The most effective protection was heavier, more permanent track—heavier rail, deeper ballast, larger tie plates, and larger ties. As locomotive design progressed, this heavier track was also favored by engineers planning heavier, higher-speed trains. In the 1920s all elements of the structure were improved. Outlays for tie plates and spikes were increased substantially in the period 1915–1920, and in the 1920s more was spent on heavier rail and more ballast (see figs. 19 and 20). Improvements in ties do not show up plainly in total outlays, because the money saved by buying fewer ties tended to offset the cost of higher investment per tie for wood preserving and seasoning (inventory). The average size of crossties was increased at small added cost. The Moss Tie Company reported that the average size of ties handled in their yards and treating plants increased from 2.67 cubic feet in 1917 to 3.2 cubic feet in 1932–1933 (about 20 percent by volume). The probable service life of the ties was lengthened by the investments in plates, rail, and ballast. The Burlington, for example, increased the size of tie plates from 6 by 8.5 inches standard in 1924–1925, to 7 by 9 inches, and by 1935 to 7.5 by 10.5 inches. The main line was entirely plated by 1929.

The third major source of innovation was the relative shift in prices of labor and materials. As described earlier, the Railroad Administration increased railroad wages dramatically. This was the beginning of a long trend in railroad maintenance toward emphasis on labor costs. Labor saving became a significant factor in decisions about research and innovation.[5]

At the end of World War I, for example, the combination of car shortages and the much higher cost of repairing railroad cars caused associations of railway engineers and car builders to treat repairs as a problem and analyze the failures that brought cars into the shop. At the end of 1918 von Schrenk was pointing out possible economies in car manufacture and repair. The railroads could make cars last and yet pay less for materials if they would specify appropriate kinds of wood

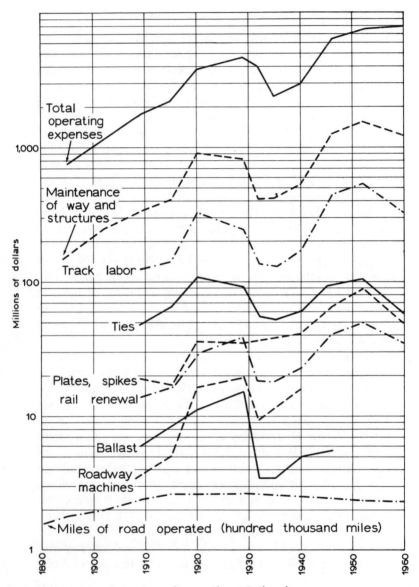

19. Maintenance of Way Expenditures, Class 1 Railroads

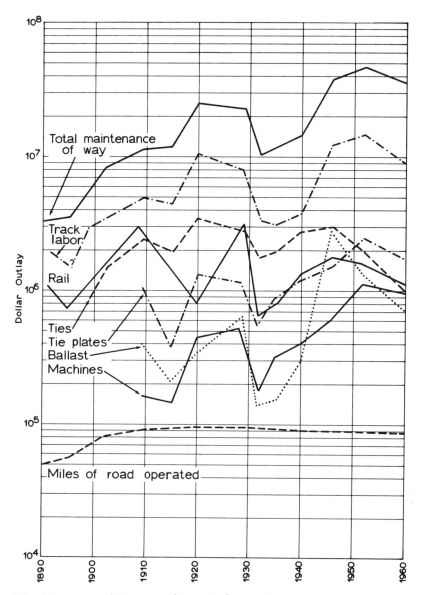

20. Maintenance of Way Expenditures, Burlington Lines

(higher strength for stress members such as posts and braces, cheaper species for unstressed parts) and if they would specify certain densities of pine lumber instead of "Georgia pine" or "longleaf." Chemical treatment would be economical for parts subjected to moisture (sills, flooring, and posts of stock cars, perhaps roofs of refrigerator cars). Much car material was serving only three or four years before it had to be replaced, and the cost of labor for replacing specific parts was large and rising. In spite of a rapid shift from all-wood to all-metal and part-metal cars before the war, in 1918 something like two billion board feet of lumber went into car construction and repair—roughly 10 percent of all construction lumber, or 4 percent of the timber harvest, or 50 percent of the amount used for crossties. About half was southern pine and Douglas fir, about one-fourth oak.

The remarkable thing is that all of those principles of economy of car construction, recommended in 1918, were standard practices of bridge construction in the late 1890s and of crosstie handling well before the war. In 1918 only two railroads (the Burlington and the Santa Fe) were treating any car lumber.[6] The cost of labor and the pressure of the car shortage (costs of downtime) provided the incentives needed to apply analytic methods and general knowledge of lumber economy to the particular field of car construction.

In the area of bridge timber, the value of preframing was described above as related to efficient chemical preserving. But the rising cost of labor added another critical incentive to prefabrication of bridge members. More machinery could be used in the shop than on the site. For example, the Reading Railroad estimated the cost of preframing at $3.50 per thousand board feet in 1923. This added about 20 percent to the cost of the timber, but all of that was recovered in savings on labor at the construction site.

In track maintenance, the cost of labor rose more than the

cost of any other inputs between 1915 and 1920. The immediate response of the railroads was to invest new sums in roadway machines and small tools (see accounts graphed in fig. 19). By the late 1920s several large mechanical ballast cleaners had been designed and were in operation. The use of more ballast and the practice of cleaning it mechanically improved drainage and resilience of the roadbed, thus extending the life of crossties. But the governing factor in the design and purchase of the machines was the need to save labor. This early mechanization of track work was so successful that from 1920 to 1929 track labor costs were more effectively controlled than any other inputs.

The new importance of labor costs is also shown in the rejection of the screw spike. Most American railroad spikes are nails, but certain European lines have long used a threaded type. Various bolt and clip-type fasteners were invented before the war, and screw spikes were recommended to reduce "spike kill" of ties. Twenty-seven out of twenty-nine railroads polled favored them. By 1919 tests on the Pennsylvania Railroad showed that screw spikes increased maintenance labor cost from one-third to two-thirds and reduced the speed of repair work after accidents, fires, and washouts. Fifty-two out of fifty-eight railroads promptly admitted that, although they had never used or tested screw spikes conclusively, they were no longer interested.

All innovations that extended the life of materials contributed to economies of labor, since most track, bridge, and car department labor or "maintenance" consisted of replacing and repairing defective materials and parts. It is not clear precisely to what extent labor costs contributed to the incentives to adopt wood preserving, seasoning, or generally heavier track, but the four examples given above—preframing of bridge timber, grading and treating of car lumber, mechanical ballast cleaning, and rejection of screw spikes

—demonstrate the growing importance of labor costs in decisions about innovation in all maintenance departments, that is, all railroad departments that used large amounts of timber.

The Supply of Railway Timber

In the 1920s, when railroad demand for timber began to decline perceptibly, there seems to have been a significant expansion of supply. From the railroad consumer's point of view, this expansion was comparable to that of the 1870s and 1880s. Once again, the major factors were technological changes that permitted hauling from new territory and utilization of new species.

The use of motor trucks and improvement of roads opened new regions. The average haul in the late 1920s was ten or eleven miles to the rail line or water instead of the five or six miles before World War I, with no apparent increase in cost. Truck haul also permitted middlemen (tie contractors) to buy from small mills and sell from large, centrally located yards. The gasoline engine made possible more efficient "portable" mills that could operate in isolated areas of rugged terrain, or move from one small woodlot to another. From the consumer's point of view, any saving in production was equivalent to increased supply, that is, more timber was offered at a given price.

The extension of wood-preserving know-how to new species and new regions also increased the supply. Untreated, the mixed hardwoods, sappy pines, and Douglas fir had small value as ties or bridge timber. Treated, their service value for ties and many items of car lumber was roughly equal to the best white oak. For bridge timber and stress members of cars, more precise specifications of quality of the piece of wood (density, permissible knots, and so forth) also allowed substitution of high-grade pieces of all those species. In other words, progressive utilization by the consumer was a factor enlarging his supply as well as reducing his consumption.

By introducing treatment and taking advantage of motor transport, many railroads were able to abandon long hauls of ties and fill their entire order from local markets. The New Haven, the New York Central, the Delaware, Lackawanna and Western, and the Milwaukee, for example, built treating plants in the 1920s and began to purchase all ties from the mixed hardwoods (maple, birch, beech). These supplies previously had been untouched along their own lines. They cooperated with local suppliers by organizing markets for tie siding (side boards). Prompt payment for ties provided working capital to local suppliers, and the railroads agreed to accept a "normal run" of grades and sizes of ties.

Purchasing records on the Burlington also indicate improved conditions of supply in the 1920s and into the 1930s. The Burlington had the facilities for treating almost any species. During the shipping crisis of 1918–1920, the line used exceptional numbers of softwood ties (a million of southern yellow pine and western yellow pine in 1920) and developed techniques for seasoning and treating cypress piling. But after the shipping crisis ceased about 1922, cypress was abandoned, and the Burlington went back to using pine piling. The line gradually reduced its purchases of southern yellow pine ties to virtually none after 1928. All those changes were in the direction of higher-quality ties and timbers. Douglas fir ties from the Inland Empire were discontinued in favor of the coastal Douglas fir in spite of higher shipping costs from the coast. The specifications for Douglas fir bridge stress members were tightened in 1931. In 1919 and again in 1933 the Burlington discussed the possibility of developing production of on-line ties in the Black Hills. The railroad was not prepared in 1919 to offer prices that would cover added costs of cutting, under Forest Service rules, from the Black Hills National Forest. It was cheaper to buy and haul Douglas fir from the West Coast. It became apparent during discussions in 1933 that the Burlington preferred off-line buying to guaranteeing a steady market. In other words, timber supply in Burlington territory was abundant, but demand was too small and sporadic to permit efficient commercial manufacture.

Forestry? Yes and No

In the mid-1920s another important source of supply was discovered. Timber had been growing unnoticed on timberland where tie cuts were made before the war. Now there were more ties. The crosstie industry discovered what one spokesman called "reforestation unpremeditated."[7]

The tie companies habitually purchased modest acreages of second-growth stumpage that had already been logged for lumber, staves, and veneer manufacture (higher-value products from the large trees). They cut the remaining trees over twelve to fourteen inches in diameter for ties, and they held onto the land. Although it took forty or fifty years for trees to grow from seed to that size, trees of tie size could be cut every ten, fifteen, or twenty years, and the forest yielded seventy-five or one hundred ties per acre at each cut. The forest was never destroyed, the trees reproduced mainly by sprouting from the stumps, and no plantings were necessary. The difference between these yields and those Andrew Fuller believed possible (see Chapter 3) is dramatic.

The practice differed from the Forest Service' conception of forestry chiefly in that the tie producers cut younger, and therefore smaller, trees than the Forest Service approved. Larger trees were valued for high-grade lumber, and it cost more to make ties from large trees than small ones. The companies practicing this type of management showed an active interest in forest legislation, forest products research, and wood utilization. In Missouri they formed the Missouri Forestry Association and drafted forest conservation legislation. Although they were influenced by the threat of government forestry and sentimental conservation, their own conception of forestry evolved mainly from their experience. The producers were interested in the business from stumpage production to service life of their product, and therefore they sought at the same time to protect their sources and their markets.

E. E. Pershall and Howard Andrews conducted influential experiments. Under the management of Pershall, the Moss Tie Company in 1922 or 1923 purchased 103,000 acres in Missouri, all of which would be for the production of ties and tie siding in the form of one-inch boards eight feet long. Producers used portable mills powered by gasoline tractors. Tie hackers or hewers were also employed. The company expected to retain and reforest the land. It already owned treating plants with large sawmills and 46,000 acres of other land in Missouri as well as tracts outside the state. By 1928 it had purchased another 140,000 acres on the Tennessee and Cumberland rivers. The company was obtaining every fifteen years on oak and every seven years on pine a cut as large as seventy-five ties per acre. Because the same company operated wood-preserving plants, it could use the several oaks and other hardwood species that occurred mixed in natural stands and the lower grades of yellow pine that grew rapidly. "Reforestation is easy for tie producers, merely an equation of interest charges and taxes against stumpage values and annual increments of growth."[8]

Andrews, who became president of the Railway Tie Association in 1925, had been producing ties in Kentucky and Tennessee for forty years. In 1925 he claimed that, in his experience, land on which oak timber grew naturally would produce seventy-five to one hundred ties per acre every twenty years, "better ties than ever before." He did not actually use the expression "sustained yield." Most ties were cut from wild second growth. Over 80 percent of ties, Andrews estimated, were cut from trees that produced a single tie each. The markets for hardwood siding were essential to this type of operation. Andrews urged the railroads to develop new markets and uses for siding and to consider forestry of this kind as traffic development. The value of a carload of ties was roughly equal to the freight on its shipment from a Tennessee producing point to a Pittsburgh consuming district. Other tie producers acquired timber to ensure their supply several years into the future, cut it selectively, and then found it possible to cut more later.[9]

Conditions of expanded supply and reduced demand allowed railroad men to dismiss the notion of depletion and to concentrate on efficient utilization. Conservation discussions were suspended during the war, and afterward they no longer fascinated railroad engineers. In 1923 the AREA Tie Committee reported that the substitution of one wood for another was cheaper than substitution of any other material. Ernest Sterling, still the most influential railroad forestry consultant in the 1920s, described ties as low-grade material that could be cut from small trees and produced on any scale of operation.

> The range and character of tie production is much broader than any other form of woods operation, save possibly acid wood or pulpwood. These conditions make practically the entire forest region a tie-producing territory with every woodlot owner or man with an axe and team a possible producer . . . With enough ties in sight to provide for the diminishing requirements resulting from preservative treatment, for more years than anyone is able to estimate and with the standing tie material within reach, supplemented by additional timber as transportation facilities

expand and new regions become exploitable, there is no apparent ground for worry or alarm. The problems for the present are in operating, distribution, and cost . . . ties will continue to come for an indefinite period from the same source they have in the past and that there is no ground for anticipating a shortage.[10]

Pershall, as a representative of tie producers, argued the same point. "Well informed leaders in our industry are not half so much concerned about a diminishing supply of good ties as they are about a decreased demand due to progress that has been made toward increased life of the tie in the track . . . The future supply has been anticipated."[11]

Thanks to the longer life of ties and the satisfactory anticipation of supply, railroad men in the 1920s refused to accept the proposals of the extremists among foresters. Plantations, forest management by railroads, and tropical woods were all rejected as sources of tie supply because the potential gains were limited to one element of cost (timber), and they required long-term large investments with high risks. As described earlier, they preferred technical alternatives that would produce savings on many factors (labor, steel, timber, capital, and so on) and that required limited investments and lower risk and could be modified over shorter intervals.

One of the extreme proposals was for imports of tropical woods for ties. Major George P. Ahern, an ally of Pinchot, was concerned with a Tropical Plant Research Foundation. Samuel J. Record proposed tropical hardwoods for railroad uses, and the American Society of Mechanical Engineers authorized study of the potential tropical supply.[12] The railway engineers were skeptical, however. The Tie Committee discussed the issue in 1922 and in 1925 strongly rejected it.

When a promoter of tropical woods hears that the railroads in the U.S. use about 110 million ties annually, that the forests producing them are being rapidly depleted, and that the prices are high, he concludes at once that there must be a sure outlet for his woods in the form of ties for use in the U.S. He soon discovers that there are more than 70 different kinds of wood in this country which are being accepted . . . The demand has never exceeded the supply . . . Prices are less than he anticipated. Railroads are not interested where there are no data on fitness. It is safe to predict that another 20 years will pass before American capital will become interested in so speculative a venture as a tropical tie operation.[13]

The plantation experiments were all abandoned at this time. The eucalyptus groves of the Santa Fe were eventually opened as exclusive homesites under a "protective covenant plan."[14] No ties were ever harvested from the Pennsylvania plantations, and by 1955 most of the properties had been sold. "It may be stated that the result of the plantations on the supply of timber to the Railroad has been negligible."[15] The PRR watershed properties under forest management were also sold off gradually as the use of diesel locomotives reduced the need for pure water. By 1927 the Delaware and Hudson had restocked 12,500 acres and set a million trees, but the company saw no markets or profits in sight. The forester tried muskrat farming, filbert nut culture, and even expressed hope for a renaissance of charcoal burning.[16]

The Burlington continued to revise expectations toward higher costs and longer rotations—forty years instead of twenty-five (see table 5).

When Besler died, J. H. Waterman, Superintendent of Timber Preservation, took charge of the catalpa plantations. In 1922 he decided not to plant any more trees because it did not pay on land valued at over five dollars per acre. "In my observation, I have been led to believe that no railroad can afford to

Table 5. Expected returns from catalpa plantations, Burlington Lines, 1921, in dollars per acre.

Rotation:	40 years		
Yield:	801 ties per acre		
Interest rate:	5 percent		
Cost to Jan. 1, 1921		115.00	
Returns expected immediately (1921)			
posts at 30 cents	320.00		
Returns, 40 years (1946)			
ties at $1, posts at 30 cents	760.00		
		1080.00	
Net return			965.00
Net value in 1921 (present value)			810.00
Costs not accounted:			
Cost of land	120.00		
Interest to 1921	122.00		
Actual returns of 1921 (half			
expected)	160.00		
		402.00	

Source: Audit of Jan. 1, 1921, MS, File CB&Q G Catalpa 1560, Burlington Lines, Galesburg, Illinois. The figures apply to the Pacific Junction plantation, eighty acres remaining. The costs not accounted were calculated from earlier data; see Table 3 for earlier expectations.

set groves of any kind expecting to get their future supplies of ties . . . [The] only people that can afford to re-forrest [*sic*] are the State or the U.S. Government. They can afford to wait." [17] The capital investment was $24,000 excluding interest, and the annual cost for care amounted to at least $1,200 a year, including forty to sixty man-days of section labor "trimming them up." In 1926 Waterman recognized the trees were crooked, wormy, and would yield small amounts of poor-quality timber. If the timber were used for railroad purposes, catalpa would need treatment. The Pacific Junction grove was finally cut. Only thirty-five ties were secured from the whole eighty acres, and they were mostly culls, that is, below the standard size or quality acceptable for purchase. Several thousand fence posts of poor quality were treated and distributed to fill roadmasters' orders for wood, steel, and concrete posts. The substitution evoked protest, and the returns scarcely paid for treatment, much less harvesting and handling. The investment at Pacific Junction was roughly $30,000 out of pocket, or $50,000 with interest charges, and the investment in all groves was double this—$100,000. Because the outlays appeared on the System Stock Report as an asset, the plantations seemed to be valuable when in fact they were white elephants. The loss was not charged off until 1956. Most of the small groves are still in existence; the trees are ten to forty-five feet tall, some as large as fourteen inches in diameter. Because of their poor form they are not worth felling and preparing even for the lowest grades of use, patching coal cars or filling in tunnels behind the lining.

Crosstie producers were discovering forestry at the very time the railroads rejected it, but there is no real contradiction here. The success of the crosstie men in their "reforestation unpremeditated" depended on certain conditions of location and management: minimum input of labor, land of low value, cheap river transport from timberland to market, consumer demand for a high-quality product, and highly specialized business organization. They were taking advantage of nature's own forestry at rigorously selected locations. They interfered little in forest growth, but instead manipulated the product to a high degree. The railroads, in abandoning their old plantations, recognized the same principles. The plantations were unsuccessful attempts to improve on the growth of natural forests of diverse local species. The railroads found they could not cheaply plant and grow a standard ready-to-use product. Even the attempts of the Pennsylvania and the Delaware and

Hudson lines to "manage" forests did not meet the rigorous requirements of location and organization for profitable lumber or crosstie production. Both the successful discoveries of the crosstie men and the failures of the railroad experiments illustrated the same principles of forest economics.

A Public Policy of Utilization

The Forest Service modified its conception of utilization during the 1920s, but continued to stress timber depletion. These two key policies were somewhat contradictory, and the balance between them was continually shifting.

Depletion, the physical shrinking of supply, remained the cornerstone of all Forest Service policies and economic theory. Lumber prices rose sharply between 1915 and 1920; the Forest Service claimed depletion was the primary cause. The nation was experiencing a housing shortage, inflation, idle land, industrial dislocation, and speculation. According to the Forest Service, depletion was partly responsible. Concentration of wealth was a matter of public concern; again, the Forest Service believed depletion had fostered it. The lumber industry was suffering from declining demand owing to substitution of other building materials; depletion had forced these substitutions. The tendency to look at the economy in terms of this a priori judgment appears in publications of the Forest Service in the early 1920s.

> More idle lands, more idle men, less home ownership, and the slow throttling of the demand for lumber by the rising tide of prices will be the evidence of our failure to restore the forests . . . Directly or indirectly, every commodity of life will cost more because of the depleted supply of forest products. Every American will pay an unnecessarily large part of his income for shelter, and food, and

Chapter 7

> clothing and fuel, transportation and amusements, necessities and luxuries alike, because wood will be no longer plentiful and near at hand . . .
>
> This economic punishment will increase in severity as time goes on. There is only one way by which its pressure can be relieved and removed, and that is by growing enough timber for the national needs.[18]

Or, similarly, "In short, with the utmost that can be done many years must pass before we can make our forests produce through growth as much timber as is now yearly taken from them, and a period of shortage is inescapable." [19]

The Capper Report of 1920 was the major forestry document in this period. Its principal arguments were these: "Three-fifths of our original timber is gone . . . We are using timber four times as fast as we are growing it . . . Depletion is a contributing cause to recent high prices of forest products, and they will increase. The fundamental problem is to increase the production of timber by stopping forest devastation. The homes and industries of the U.S. require at least 35 billion feet of lumber yearly . . . A reduction in the current supply of lumber below this figure would seriously curtail our economic development . . . We cannot afford to cut our per capita use of lumber to half or one third the present amount . . ." [20] Dubious arguments were used to buttress the idea of depletion. The report contended that depletion was demonstrated by the fact that railroads that had formerly carried only small inventories of timber were now carrying six to nine months' supplies. That change was, in fact, due to the introduction of sensible methods of seasoning, which reduced railroad maintenance costs and were not related to the availability of timber. Although depletion ought to affect the price of stumpage, as figure 21 shows, the price of crosstie stumpage did not increase

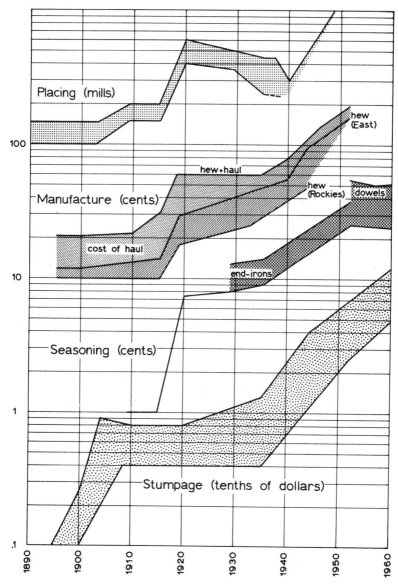

Placing (mills)

hew
(East)

hew+haul

Manufacture (cents)

hew
(Rockies)

dowels

cost of haul

end-irons

Seasoning (cents)

Stumpage (tenths of dollars)

100

10

1

.1

1890 1900 1910 1920 1930 1940 1950 1960

21. Variation of Crosstie Costs

during the war or in the 1920s; the increases in cost of ties lay primarily in added labor costs. But the Capper Report showed price trends graphically without relation to price levels for other commodities or factors such as labor.

Much of this thinking was based on a report of the Bureau of Corporations, which studied speculation and concentration in the lumber industry about 1913. The bureau had based its estimates of consumption and forest growth on Forest Service estimates. The reports were a house of cards; each was built upon the assumptions of the previous reports. "The present annual growth is estimated by the Forest Service at only about one third the annual cut . . . Because of this fact that standing timber is a natural resource constantly diminishing in amount, its value would naturally tend to increase, even if there were no pronounced concentration of ownership . . . The interest on the present value of a supply of standing timber for such a period as twenty or thirty years would be prohibitive, of course, were it not for the rapidly rising value of the standing timber itself. For many years the value of timber has been rising rapidly, so that it has been highly profitable to hold mature timber merely for the increase in price."[21] Rolf Thelen's report on substitution as a factor in the unhealthy lumber economy, owing to timber shortage, was also an outgrowth of investigations by the Bureau of Corporations. "The timber shortage which has followed the exhaustion of the local supply has been one of the causes of high lumber prices and the decreasing use of wood. The total consumption of wood is far in excess of the growth . . . There are very direct relations between increasing substitution, and decreasing relative demand for lumber, intense competition among lumber producers, price limitations set by actual or potential competition from substitutes, recurring overproduction of lumber and price fluctuations, and general instability within the lumber industry."[22]

The threat of depletion was the "big stick" behind the policy of balancing growth against drain. This theory or policy would be called "sustained-yield forestry." The equilibrium was conceived in terms of a simple equation of quantities, not in terms of economic equilibrium. "In short, with the utmost that can be done many years must pass before we can make our forests produce through growth as much timber as is now yearly taken from them, and a period of shortage is inescapable." [23]

Meanwhile, the Forest Service attached new meaning to the term "utilization." Utilization was an idea current among European foresters by the eighteenth century, but it has not always meant the same things to everyone. In 1911 utilization studies of the Forest Service were simply statistics of consumption. There was no attempt to analyze the value of alternative uses. From 1915 the Forest Service interpreted utilization as seeking markets or uses for low-grade materials. The Forest Products Laboratory was directed to concentrate on problems of administration of the National Forests. One such problem, for example, was the lack of uses for small or defective trees derived from thinning or improvement cuts. The Forest Service meant physical, not economic, use. They sought ways to expand low-value uses for such things as thinnings and logging wastes, without reference to expanding the net product, which an economist would measure in terms of its value.

Between 1920 and 1925 the annual reports of the Forester spoke more and more urgently about waste, the waste of unproductive land and the waste of wood in lumbering, fires, and manufacturing. The Forest Products Laboratory was directed "to do by saving what silviculture does by timbergrowing . . . Wood saved is equivalent to wood grown." [24] Recognition of utilization as of equal importance with silviculture was an important step; it justified more forest products research, a new building for the products laboratory at Madison (completed in 1932), and cooperation with lumbermen and consumers. Increasing emphasis on utilization was a move in the direction of a more rational conservation policy.

There were several reasons for the new emphasis on utilization. The expansion of the Forest Products Laboratory during World War I gave it more weight in the policy of the Forest Service. The discovery just before the war that the lumber industry was economically unhealthy prompted a change of attitude toward the manufacturers; they could no longer be regarded as simple villains of timber depletion. The manufacturers themselves began to pay attention to utilization problems, and the Department of Commerce played an important role in fostering cooperation and utilization studies.

The demands of defense research on packaging, glues, and airplane woods permitted a fivefold expansion of the funds and personnel at the Forest Products Laboratory. Results of wartime projects were available for industrial development after the war. The new facilities were converted to civilian use not merely to perpetuate a remarkable operation, but to boost the American economy. The value of the laboratory to the war effort and to postwar commerce was recognized at this time and gave the institution more leverage in formulating forest policy. The laboratory personnel were engineers and chemists by training; few had come into the laboratory from silviculture. They were active in the engineering associations and represented the views of consumers and manufacturers, the users of timber. Their approach consistently showed a greater grasp of economic realities than the rest of the Forest Service.

Thelen's report of 1917 on substitution, for example, presented an engineer's view. Like Fernow in the 1890s and like contemporary spokesmen for the wood preservers and lumber manufacturers, he viewed substitution as a result of relative price changes. He distinguished between a unit cost from the producer's viewpoint and a cost in place or cost for a given service from the consumer's point of view. He argued that research was the means to reduce production costs and permit more economical use of material by the consumer. Research that made wood more useful would protect the threatened markets for that product. In his interpretation, "utilization" and "utility" refer to the consumer's costs, techniques, and interests.

> In their efforts to create new fields and to enter fields already occupied, the substitute industries have been compelled to offer increased service in the form of exact data regarding the properties of their materials. Some of these industries have therefore expended large sums in scientific study of properties and processes and the best methods of *utilization,* and in attempts to improve the quality of their products. For lumber and other wood products similar information has been comparatively lacking . . . The entire situation in these respects has been a potent cause of substitution.
>
> Utility or service depends in part upon the inherent properties of the materials themselves and the extent to which these properties can be improved through scientific development. In part it depends also upon manufacturing specifications [grading rules], adherence in manufacture . . . and extent to which properties . . . are made common knowledge among consumers.
>
> Ordinarily competition centers upon the initial and ultimate cost of construction, and accepted beliefs as to the *utility* of different materials [italics mine].[25]

While Aldo Leopold was associated with the Forest Products Laboratory, he espoused this view of utilization and demonstrated that more efficient utilization and product research could make forestry profitable. Foresters in the past had urged patience; they said the price of stumpage would rise, and forestry would eventually become profitable. Leopold, in an article written in 1927, argued that this could not be expected to happen automatically. The competition of substitute materials set a ceiling on the price of wood. At the same time, the cost of growing or even holding timber set a floor under prices. "The margin of profit on which commercial forestry depends must be found somewhere between that floor and that ceiling. But how? The only way to find a margin of profit which does not already exist is to learn by research how to get bigger yields or better quality or both . . . The competition of substitute materials makes it necessary to look to the purposeful enhancement of wood values by research . . ."[26] Utilization of waste was only one objective of product research, "the most easily dramatized." Product research had the more important objective of enhancing the value of forest products by sorting the material to segregate the properties required for various uses and by manipulating or modifying the properties. "If we make it [wood] render better service, we add to its value, as distinguished from its price, and the price ceiling is not operative as an obstacle. . . . The variability of natural growth wood, which is a handicap can be converted into versatility, which is an asset, by means of selective tests."[27]

At the same time the Department of Commerce was pressing toward the same conception of utilization and product research. During the 1920s that department was one of the most important and positive influences on the forest economy. It was committed to an economic point of view, and it was accustomed to harmonizing diverse self-seeking interests. In these two respects it differed from the Forest Service and was thus able to complement it. As it was organized in 1921, the department had two vital concerns that were closely linked: the improvement of American foreign trade to face European economic recovery; and the "campaign for the elimination of waste," which would increase real wages through lower prices and would permit industries to survive the wage adjustments of World War I.[28] "Just as twenty years ago we undertook nation-wide conservation of natural resources, so now we must undertake nation-wide elimination of waste."[29] The Department of Commerce in the mid-1920s was able to harness public moral indignation and personal values to the economic interests of individuals and corporations making "dollars and cents contributions to the advancement of American commerce." The watchword was waste. Waste was immoral as well as expensive. The new concept of waste was even broader than the old concept of conservation. Waste was generated by depression unemployment, by the speculation and overproduction of booms, by labor conflicts and turnover, by intermittent and seasonal activities, by bottlenecks in transport, by excessive variation in products, by fire, accident, and disease. Some of these resulted from the failure of various interests to adjust themselves efficiently to each other over short periods of time.

The Department of Commerce launched a many-pronged attack on waste. The new institutions and projects affected the forest products economy and the railroad consumer as well as other timber users. Like the Forest Products Laboratory, the laboratory of the Bureau of Standards of the Department of Commerce had expanded through the crash programs of defense research. It became "the greatest physics and research laboratory in the world" (its own estimation). Wartime work developed substitutes for materials and instruments formerly imported from Europe. Important fields of research were clay products, fuels, aluminum, insulation, and fire control. After the war the bureau was directed to take advantage of its facilities to cooperate with manufacturers "with a view to assisting in the permanent establishment of new American industries developed during the war." A Building and Housing Agency (1919) fostered interest in testing and standardizing materials. The department created a Division of Simplified Practice (1921)[30] and a Federal Specifications Board (1923) and assisted in founding the American Engineering Standards Committee, on which all the engineering societies were represented.

Activities to develop exports convinced manufacturers that simplification, information, and programs of research were in their interest. The Lumber Division, headed by Axel Oxholm, published a directory, international lumber conversion tables, statistics, foreign grade markings, and so forth, in order to foster lumber exports. These activities fostered communications among lumbermen and a concern on their part for market expansion at home. The first great achievement of this program was the American Lumber Standards, the work of a Central Committee on Lumber Standards. The committee included representatives of lumber manufacturers, wholesalers, retailers, engineers and architects, and the user industries such as the railroads. The Forest Service did technical work for the committee, and the standards were based largely on the structural timber specifications of the railway engineers, the lumber classifications of the railroad car manufacturers, and the grading rules of the lumber manufacturers. The standards were then formally adopted by all the agencies, incorporated into their manuals, and widely publicized, beginning in 1923. Although these diverse groups had met occasionally, for example at the American Forest Congress in 1905 and at the National Conservation Congress in 1909, this was the first cooperation with sustained work and definite results.

In 1924 President Coolidge and Secretary of Agriculture Henry Wallace called a national conference on waste in the forest products economy. A National Committee on Wood Utilization was founded to do research on the problems presented at the mass meeting; this committee continued to operate under the aegis of the Department of Commerce.[31] A handbook published in 1929 summarizes its objectives and many of its accomplishments. "By showing how a simple unified grading of lumber recently adopted can be applied to give the wood user that kind of material which will serve his particular purpose most economically, and by setting forth the principles of efficient construction, the handbook will diminish waste and will produce a larger return from the lumber dollar . . . Herbert Hoover was its primary inspiration, and the facilities of the Department of Commerce were at the service of the Committee most liberally. The Forest Products Laboratory cooperated with readiness . . ."[32] The handbook sought to publicize fire-resistant methods of construction and the new Lumber Standards. The preparatory studies uncovered fields in which wood research lagged as compared with other materials. Instead of emphasizing depletion as negative, it emphasized the relation between past overabundance and waste, and among present moderate supplies, advancing knowledge, and economical use. Availability and research would "continue to maintain and to expand the utility and use" of wood. The statements were a careful compromise among the Forest Service, lumber producers, and consumers. Their several interpretations of utilization were reconciled in each project. For example, the committee made a survey of the lengths of lumber purchased and the lengths used, in order to find outlets for lumber of small dimension and of short and odd lengths. This would reduce physical waste as the Forest Service desired, increase manufacturers' revenues, and reduce consumers' costs.

The work of the National Committee on Wood Utilization was closely related to the revitalization of the National Lumber Manufacturers Association. Wilson Compton, the secretary and manager of the association, in an address of 1927 made a clear distinction between physical utilization and economic utilization. "The trend in the direction of small logs has gone to the extent of waste. Expenditures upon their utilization are greater than the value of the products therefrom. This to be sure is physical utilization. But it is economic waste." Compton pointed out the shortsightedness of the manufacturer who related prices of his product to his costs, but did not consider the price of his product in relation to its value to the consumer. "The lumber industry has relied on price advantage. It has not become accustomed to thinking in terms of the mechanical and physical qualities of its products and their comparison with similar characteristics of competing materials." After stating that the increase in transportation haul as well as stumpage values had destroyed the price advantage, he argued: "Profit in lumber manufacture hereafter is going to be dependent less upon lower costs and more upon higher *realization*. Lumbermen as a whole have too much figured prices as reasonable or unreasonable because of their relationship to the cost of production rather than because of the extent to which lumber has added to the value of the finished product for which the lumber is used [italics mine]." Compton proposed that product research would help diversify markets for lumber and expand higher-value uses. Diversification would also reduce seasonal and cyclical instability in the industry. To capture markets, he urged trade and grade marking and studies of the properties of wood. He presented a chart showing the extent to which mechanical, electrical, and other physical properties were unknown for various species. The lack of knowledge discouraged substitution of species and fostered substitution of other industrial materials. Control of these properties would follow. "Fire-proof, rot-proof, bug-proof and shrink-proof lumber" would be possible when the industry became as "diligent in research as many of its ardent competitors." [33]

The accuracy of Compton's estimate of the economic situation and its compatibility with thinking in related industries and among engineers in general helped to increase his impact. The National Lumber Manufacturers Association was induced to appropriate money for a laboratory, to begin cooperative work with users of wood and with the government, and to consider "design research" as well as research on the properties that could be controlled in manufacture. Design research referred to work that would "show the user how to adjust the material more economically or more effectively to his purposes."

Leopold, Compton, and Oxholm, representatives, respectively, of the Forest Products Laboratory, the National Lumber Manufacturers Association, and the Department of Commerce, were all thinking along the same lines. Utilization was the umbrella under which foresters, engineers, manufacturers, and consumers gathered. All represented a rational economic approach to conservation. All had a breadth of view of the problems of the forest products economy as a whole. All were persuaded that technical research was the chief instrument of rational conservation. From 1925 on it looked as if their insight and cooperation would modify the direction of American forestry.

Cooperation of manufacturers, consumers, laboratory engineers, and foresters created an effective political alliance to obtain funds for government forestry and forest products research. The Clark-McNary Forest Law of 1924 permitted acquisition of public forests and aid to state governments for fire control. The McSweeney-McNary Law of 1928 allocated new funds to products research.[34]

The Forester, William Greeley, was open to the views of the manufacturers, engineers, and consumers of wood. They were able in the mid-1920s to soft-pedal depletion and to introduce a greater emphasis on utilization, which tended to counterbalance depletion propaganda. Oxholm, for example, as chairman of the National Committee on Wood Utilization, objected to overemphasis on depletion as a result of too great a use of the forests. "Curtailing the use of wood does not help the cause of forest perpetuation. On the contrary, use alone can create value, and therefore non-use would remove the economic incentive to tree-growing." He obtained from Greeley a reply in which Greeley walked the tightrope. In keeping with his earlier views, Greeley balanced concepts of depletion and utilization: "Timber growing, as you point out, is primarily an economic process. If it does not pay, forests cannot be widely and generally produced. To make it pay there must be an adequate market for forest products. Hence it is clear to me that liberal use of wood will promote forestry and the profitable employment of our forest land. The constructive solution of the whole problem lies in timber use and timber culture, each backing and sustaining the other . . . Necessarily a long time will be required to work out our situation to one of real stability . . . But we can and should balance the ledger in this fashion without denying to the country a liberal use of wood . . ." [35] The annual report of 1927, which made "sustained yield the essential aim of all forestry," described products research as the "most important way to make forestry pay." [36] The 1929 report of the new Forester, Robert Stuart, recognized the abundance of low-grade materials and described products research as the way to utilize this timber and to "assure wood a leading place as a basic raw material." The language of the report implied that perpetuation of the forests was the primary object, but recognized that the development of new uses and new markets—"effective and sufficient outlets"—was the means to that end. [37]

"The Perpetual Emergency"

During the Great Depression the cooperative efforts of the 1920s collapsed in a primitive struggle for survival. Each public agency and private interest rode off in a different direction. Tie producers and railroads could not agree on market stabilization policies, their most serious unsolved problem. In 1933 the National Committee on Wood Utilization was shelved. Released from the reins of cooperation with manufacturers and consumers, the Forest Service returned to a primary emphasis on depletion.

The Forester's report for 1931 continued the approach of the 1920s. It emphasized the demoralization of the lumber industry, complete since the crash, the value of products and market development, and the role of scientific research. Thanks to the momentum of the wood utilization movement and the demands of industry, the Forest Products Laboratory moved into new facilities in 1932. However, the annual reports of

1932–1935 and *A National Plan for American Forestry* (known as the Copeland Report, 1933) placed the emphasis strongly on depletion. The idea of utilization was relegated to a division of product research. It was no longer the key idea; the "umbrella" was folded up and stored in a closet. Popular new ideas of land use, multiple use, planned development, social values for farmers, and stabilization of industry were exploited to justify forestry, and some novel ideas were presented as "economics": "One-third the area of the continental United States is forest or potential forest land. Sound economics requires that this area be so managed that it may permanently support its fair share of the Nation's population . . ."[1] "The fact that the consumption of wood, both per capita and total, has been declining in the United States over a long period of years is a challenge that must be faced and answered. Furthermore, it is urgently important, in the period of temporary scarcity of prime large timber that looms directly ahead between times of depletion and regrowth, that the smaller sizes of trees be made more serviceable through new and improved adaptations to use, so that wood shall not lose ground permanently under the competitive pressure of other materials."[2]

The Copeland Report was organized around the idea of an imbalance between forest production and the drains upon it. By concentrating on sawtimber, the report obscured the fact that overall cellulose production was roughly in balance. The assumptions made about timber use inflated drain. The Forest Service expected markets for sawtimber to expand and believed that lumber, not chemical products and pulp, would continue to make up the major "normal requirement."

The Forest Service was apparently groping for an economic definition of supply and demand, as shown in this citation from the *National Plan:*

"Requirements" is not a wholly satisfactory term to define the extent of past, present, or future use of wood. Where timber is abundant and easily accessible, "requirements" inevitably absorb a far greater quantity of this cheap and adaptable raw material than would come into demand under other circumstances; competition from other materials is reduced; substitution moves rather in the opposite direction, and wood replaces other more costly and less readily accessible materials. On the other hand, where wood is scarce and hard to get, actual use is not a measure of what requirements might be under more favorable conditions. The community or region may not consciously demand more wood and may yet be at a disadvantage in a number of ways through lack of an abundant supply of wood at hand.[3]

The plan proposed extension of public ownership of forest lands and public control of cutting. "The problem is basically one of correcting the defects in the distribution of forest ownership." Money was requested for more research in silviculture, and the continuation of products research was justified on the grounds that the government had an enormous investment in the National Forests, half a billion dollars on the stump. The report set the tone for New Deal conservation and alarmist interpretations by those who did not read between the lines. Joseph Eastman, for example, the new Federal Co-ordinator of Transportation, predicted, on the basis of that report, a rising cost of crosstie timber owing to serious depletion. He interpreted the current overproduction as "technical" and urged the railroads to reconsider substitute ties of metal and concrete.[4]

As the Forest Survey, a census of standing timber, began to yield information, the growth rates were found to be greater and consumption smaller than was formerly believed.[5] "Depletion" simply did not exist, but the Forest Service continued to preach it. In the Forester's report of 1937 the slogan was "An economy of scarcity with respect to forests is unsafe." [6] The report of 1938 admitted that the Capper Report (1920) and the Copeland Report had overstated the imminence of a general timber shortage. The slogan that year was, nevertheless, "We Need More Forests." Need was divorced from any concept of demand. "Consumption of forest products often bears little relation to real needs for them. This is true of wood used for construction and upkeep of residences and farm buildings, by railroads, industries, and the like . . ." [7] In 1939 the language was modified: "the drain from *usable* forests exceeds their growth [italics mine] . . ." The grounds for the depletion argument had been cut away by the observations of the Forest Survey, but the dead horse was still being beaten. ". . . remaining *accessible* virgin timber may be gone before enough *usable* second growth to meet *real* needs becomes available . . . As a Nation we would be better off with more rather than fewer forests. This is true whether or not markets for more forest products are in sight [italics mine]." Declining consumption was attributed to depletion. "Fortunately all analyses indicate that needs for lumber and other forest products are much greater than the quantity that has actually been used annually during the past decade." [8]

Private and Railroad Forestry

In the mid-1930s the pulpwood industry was expanding into the southern pine region. The Forest Service regarded this as a threat to the forest because small trees, down to four inches in diameter, might be cut for pulp. Even the tie producers, consumers of trees down to ten or eleven inches in diameter, were alarmed, because they found that their supply would be depleted, in Louisiana and East Texas, for example. In 1937 the Southern Pulpwood Conservation Association was formed, to practice "self-control" which would forestall threatened public control. The tie producers joined the effort and urged the railroads also to support the conservation activities of the pulp producers.[9]

In the late 1930s other producers in the southern pine region began to consider forestry practices. The threat of federal control was an incentive, and the gradual discovery of the profitable, rapid growth rates of southern forests was another. The integration of forest products industries—naval stores, lumber, ties, pulp, distillation—made it possible to make a piece of timberland productive over a long interval. An example was the Superior Pine Company which purchased the Suwanee forest (208,000 acres) in 1925 and by the mid-1930s was practicing integrated forest products management, including production of crossties.[10] Firms concerned with long-term holding of forestland were interested in sustained yield, utilization for products of the highest value, and silvicultural as well as economic information that would permit highest returns.

"Industrial forestry" had been boosted by the Society of American Foresters for at least a decade, and in the late 1930s some believed the day of forestry had arrived. Progress was in fact very modest. Sterling observed in 1938 at the SAF meeting: "After years of effort the question of how forestry can be made to pay, and how to make feasible the things that should be done still remains unanswered . . . A combination of economics, silviculture, time, and viewpoint need a lot of cooking before they will jell." He recognized that the lumber industry had not taken over the job of growing timber, but "it is doubtful if foresters were prepared to handle the economic aspects of the problem." He questioned the need to produce the kind of timber that filled the nation's earlier needs. "Moreover, if the policies advocated became effective in a large measure, it is quite likely that overproduction of wood will be a problem for future foresters . . . Costs and more costs are the first things industry wants to know . . . This is the opportunity, but we should not fool ourselves that industry is ready or forestry is prepared to go all the way in applying this economic relationship." [11]

From 1937 the Seaboard Air Line railroad was prominent among the industrial foresters in the South. The object was the traffic that would be generated by hauling timber and wood products to market. The railroad promoted fire control and encouraged forest users to acquire timberlands. The railroad's agricultural department encouraged cropping and selective cutting. The railroad assisted in market development, that is, the creation of wood-consuming industries along the line. Railroad representatives argued that forestry practices in the area were actually ahead of industrial market opportunities. Their appraisal of the economics of the forest industry was more realistic than was customary among foresters.

The railroads of the nation aligned themselves with the interests of private forest owners in regions where private ownership was large, and with public forestry in regions of recreation and tourism. This inconsistency stemmed from the primary concern for railroad traffic. Future timber supply to the railroads themselves was not an issue because hardwoods for ties were plentiful, and competing uses for hardwoods had declined. The map of crosstie prices in 1937 (fig. 22) illustrates the continuing importance of the Tennessee and Mississippi valley hardwood supply and the demands of the high-density rail network of the manufacturing belt. The market geography in the eastern and central U.S. differed little in 1937 from that of 1882 (see figs. 2 and 3), or that of the 1960s. Douglas fir was plentiful for bridge timber, and the supply of southern

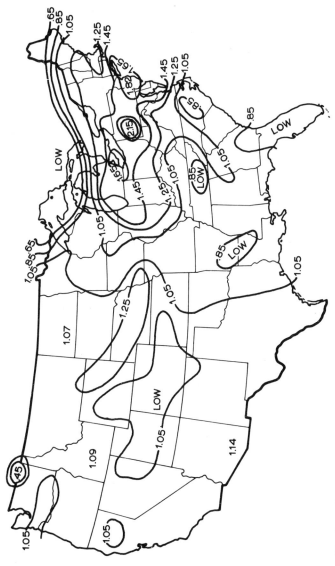

22. Crosstie Prices, 1937, Dollars per Untreated Crosstie

yellow pine appeared more elastic and growth rates higher than the experts had formerly believed.

The wartime experience of the 1940s was much like that of the period 1918-1920: rapidly rising labor costs, increasing urban job opportunities, and development of new uses for wood, such as plywood and paper products, and temporary efforts to save metals by substituting wood. The net effects of those pressures were shortages of timber and rising prices for forest products. But the higher prices and new uses made the prospects of the wood industries appear much brighter. Better market prospects provided the incentive to conduct forest products research after the war and to invest in timberland and timber management. New fiscal arrangements also overcame one of the chief obstacles to tree farming—the capital gains tax. This tax, which had encouraged owners to sell their timber rather than cut it themselves, was revised in 1943 to favor holding timber. "The 1943 Capital Gains Amendment to the Internal Revenue Code (Section 117(K)) is considered one of the very great stimuli to the practice of sound, profitable forestry. The legislation ... recognizes the financial yield of stumpage as capital gains with a lower tax rate than on ordinary income." [12]

The American Forest Products Industries, Inc., was organized in 1941 and expanded during and after the war, around the "tree farming" idea. Many Tree Farms were owned by large, vertically integrated expanding industries that did considerable research. One of the usual objectives was an improved public image for the firms. Many railroads took land they already held and reorganized their management practices to meet Tree Farm standards. They determined to take advantage of their holdings, usually with the purpose of promoting traffic development, as in the 1930s. Like the prairie lines that did agricultural extension work and tree planting in the 1870s to promote land sales and develop revenue traffic, major railroads in the 1940s and 1950s began to pursue policies of developing forest products traffic on a long-range, sustained basis. Competition from trucking stimulated a concern with traffic comparable to the initial period of railroad expansion with its vigorous competition among the transcontinental systems.

The new effort generally took place in the forested areas of fast growth, chiefly the Pacific Northwest and the southern pine region. The exception was the Chicago and Northwestern Railroad, which continued to promote shelterbelt planting in the prairies, as well as pulp development in Wisconsin. The large southeastern lines, notably the Seaboard Air Line, the Illinois Central, Atlantic Coast Line, and Central of Georgia, promoted fire protection, espoused the idea of timber cropping, and operated model forests and demonstration trains. The former land-grant railroads and their subsidiaries in the Pacific Northwest (the Northern Pacific, the Southern Pacific Land Company, and the Milwaukee Land Company) stopped selling off their timberland outright; instead, they began to sell only timber and to promote fire protection and reseeding, in the interest of future revenues from forest products traffic.

Crossties were definitely a negligible factor in this forestry effort. Only the Northern Pacific claimed in 1945 to contemplate managing part of its extensive timberlands as Tree Farms for long-term railroad tie supply to its Paradise, Montana, treating plant. The Northern Pacific has never, in practice, filled its timber requirements to any substantial degree from the harvest from its own lands.[13]

The process of vertical integration continued in the forest products industries, and the large integrated firm contributed to progress of both product research and private forestry. Taylor-Colquitt, for example, which owned forests and wood-preserving plants in the South, created a subsidiary firm,

Ta-Co, which developed commercial "vapor drying" for railroad ties. The Koppers Company acquired large timber stands and numerous wood-preserving plants. It already produced steel products and was a large manufacturer of creosote and other tar and chemical products. Koppers introduced forest management, met Tree Farm standards for large acreages, and contributed to research on artificial seasoning and preservatives.

From the early 1930s to the present, much of the increased efficiency of the forest products industries and the greater profitability of long-term forest management must be attributed at least partly to the tying together of timber management, the manufacturing of a greater variety of products, and the further processing (seasoning, treating) of a higher-value product.

Utilization on the Railroads

The general adoption of preservative treatment of crossties and investments in heavier track in the 1920s paid off in the 1930s, and railroads were able to cut their crosstie budgets by one-third during the critical years of the depression. Wood-preserving plants operated at levels as low as 20 to 25 percent of capacity.[14] Engineers feared that some of the reduction was mere postponement of work, and some was a temporary cutback because of less traffic and wear, but they found later that they had underestimated the genuine long-run economies realized through greater efficiency.[15] During the heavy traffic of World War II volumes of crosstie and bridge timber purchased did not return to former levels. Indeed, they did not increase at all, and after the war they again began to decline (see fig. 26).

By World War II the railroads had so far reduced their requirements for ties and bridge timber that railroad timber became a mere specialty of lumber manufacture and wood-preserving industries. The Office of Price Administration found that in every region of the U.S. tie prices had to be pegged to lumber prices because all but 15 to 25 percent of ties were made in diversified sawmills. By the 1950s many railroads reorganized their distribution systems to eliminate some of their treating plants. Some were sold; others were dismantled. The Burlington, for example, abolished the Sheridan plant and centralized all wood preservation at Galesburg in 1956. In 1955 the Southern Railway began to purchase treated ties as a finished product. Up to that time, all ties were purchased and treated to special order or treated in railroad plants.

In addition to payoffs from earlier innovations, what factors have contributed to ever longer life of crossties since the 1930s? As preservation reduced losses from decay, more attention was paid to problems of mechanical stresses or wear on crossties. Part of the solution lay in heavier track structure, a long-term trend. But it will be shown that the chief incentive to reduce renewals of ties was not economy of wood. Technical relationships among all parts of track structure meant that savings of various factors of production were also interrelated; a complex of technical changes produced a whole set of new economies.

One significant change was the gradual substitution of hardwood ties for softwoods (fig. 18) because the hardwoods held up longer under the heavier and faster trains. But the use of hardwoods required more attention to problems of splitting and checking, which became the major cause of removal of ties. Splitting and checking of a piece of wood result from the internal stresses produced by uneven loss of moisture during seasoning. End-irons were used on ties to prevent splitting. Doweling, a more effective method, was first introduced in 1933, and the practice spread rapidly after the Second World

War. Steel dowels of various designs may be used to reclaim ties that have split during seasoning, or "hundred percent doweling" of all ties may be used as a preventive measure.

"Artificial" seasoning with controlled temperatures and humidity and the use of chemicals promised results in limiting splitting. It also made usable certain species such as black gum and hickory. To season them in the open air, one must supervise them closely and treat them promptly when they are ready. The substitution of species continued as part of a long process of increasing flexibility. Although artificial seasoning added new capital and labor costs, it also accelerated the process and thus reduced inventory costs. For example, timber can be processed from stump to rail line in a few days or even twenty-four hours instead of a year. Some controlled seasoning in kilns was used earlier for car lumber (on the Norfolk and Western since 1915 and on the Burlington since the 1930s) and other higher-grade construction lumber, but it was first adopted commercially for crossties in 1945 (Taylor-Colquitt's "vapor drying") and first became standard practice on the Santa Fe in the 1950s.

Certain other practices of preparing and treating timbers were also related to greater use of hardwoods and the concern about splitting, checking, and mechanical wear. Petroleum solutions of creosote were preferred to straight creosote. Adzing and boring before treatment were universal by the end of the 1930s, and incising was standard practice to prepare Douglas fir for treatment.

Railroad engineers continued to strengthen all parts of the track structure: heavier rail, heavier tie plates, deeper ballast. This was necessary for new high-speed streamliners such as the Burlington Zephyr, pioneered in 1933. One element was the use of larger ties that lasted longer. The eight-foot tie was still most common in 1920, but by 1939 the tie of eight and a half feet was general on eastern lines, and the Santa Fe became the first line to adopt a nine-foot standard. This change offers clues to the motivation and complexity of track innovations. Apparently "depletion" was no longer a consideration that restrained engineers from demanding the best possible tie. The tie of eight and a half feet, which provided 17 percent more support than the eight-foot tie, cost only 5 percent more.[16] Labor costs definitely influenced the preference for longer ties. Longer ties were one way to add strength to the track. So was closer spacing of ties, but closer spacing would increase the cost of tamping ballast. The cost of track labor was decisive in this choice between alternatives. In the long run the larger tie probably lasted longer and saved wood, but that was a modest "bonus" saving.

The growing importance of labor costs in maintenance of way is revealed in the accounts. Labor costs rose with the introduction of wages and hours legislation in 1934 and skyrocketed during and immediately after World War II. Burlington accounts show a striking divergence between outlays for labor and materials, in both track maintenance and wood preserving (fig. 23). Figure 24 shows changes in unit costs of several types of maintenance of way labor and the success of one line, the Lehigh Valley, in reducing the quantities of labor required. The sharp upward movement of wages can be compared with the somewhat more moderate changes in the price of steel (fig. 25). Because labor was the major component of timber prices, unit costs of timber also rose rapidly (see fig. 26). But because total outlays of the railroads for timber were much smaller than their outlays for labor, the rising cost of labor became their chief concern and the governing factor in innovations in the use of materials.

Stumpage was a still smaller part of the total cost of crossties. Although its price began rising in the late 1930s, its share

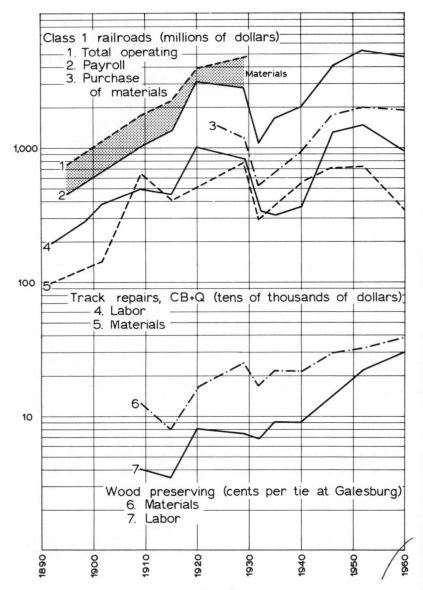

Class 1 railroads (millions of dollars)
1. Total operating
2. Payroll
3. Purchase of materials

Materials

1,000

100

Track repairs, CB+Q (tens of thousands of dollars)
4. Labor
5. Materials

10

Wood preserving (cents per tie at Galesburg)
6. Materials
7. Labor

1890 1900 1910 1920 1930 1940 1950 1960

23. Railroad Outlays for Labor and Materials

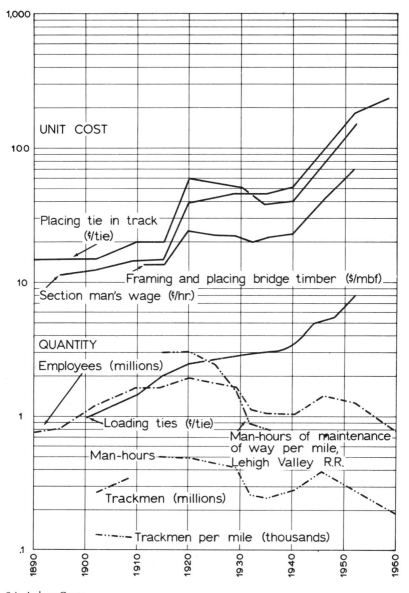

UNIT COST

Placing tie in track (¢/tie)

Framing and placing bridge timber ($/mbf)

Section man's wage (¢/hr.)

QUANTITY

Employees (millions)

Loading ties (¢/tie)

Man-hours of maintenance of way per mile, Lehigh Valley R.R.

Man-hours

Trackmen (millions)

Trackmen per mile (thousands)

24. Labor Costs

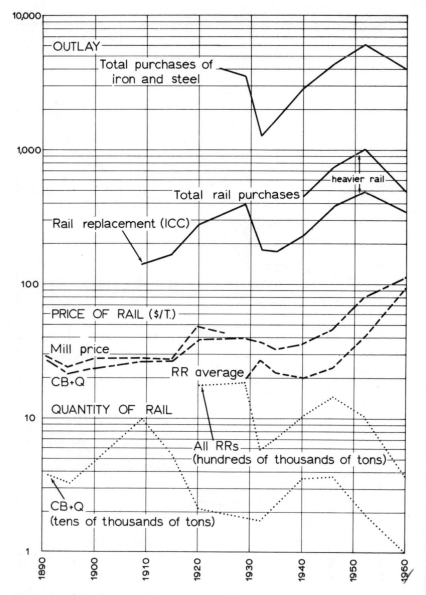

10,000

OUTLAY

Total purchases of
iron and steel

1,000

Total rail purchases

Rail replacement (ICC)

heavier rail

100

PRICE OF RAIL ($/T.)

Mill price

CB+Q

RR average

QUANTITY OF RAIL

All RRs
(hundreds of thousands of tons)

10

CB+Q
(tens of thousands of tons)

1

1890 1900 1910 1920 1930 1940 1950 1960

25. Iron and Steel Costs in Maintenance of Way

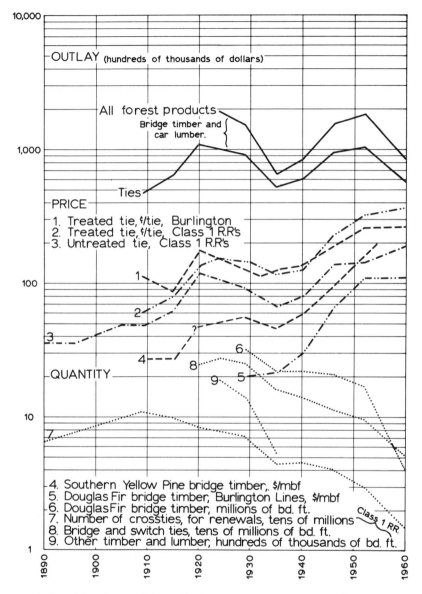

10,000

OUTLAY (hundreds of thousands of dollars)

All forest products

Bridge timber and
car lumber.

1,000

Ties

PRICE

1. Treated tie, ⊄/tie, Burlington
2. Treated tie, ⊄/tie, Class 1 R.R's
3. Untreated tie, Class 1 R.R's

1

2

3

100

?

6

4

8

QUANTITY

9   5

10

7

4. Southern Yellow Pine bridge timber, $/mbf
5. Douglas Fir bridge timber, Burlington Lines, $/mbf
6. Douglas Fir bridge timber, millions of bd. ft.
7. Number of crossties, for renewals, tens of millions
8. Bridge and switch ties, tens of millions of bd. ft.
9. Other timber and lumber, hundreds of thousands of bd. ft.

Class 1 R.R.

1

1890 1900 1910 1920 1930 1940 1950 1960

26. Railroad Purchases of Forest Products

in the total annual cost of the tie in place has continued to decline (see fig. 21). The labor costs of manufacture, treatment, and insertion in track far outweigh the raw material cost.

Mechanization is another example of the relationship between economies of labor and materials. Mechanization of work on tracks was intended to save labor. The invention and perfection of large roadway machines progressed rapidly in the 1930s, and the "account" that has grown fastest in maintenance of way departments ever since has been the outlay for roadway machines. But mechanization meant cleaner ballast, scheduled surfacing of track and therefore smoother track, more uniform wear, and longer life for ties and rail, as well as for rolling stock. The economies of timber and steel were once again a by-product of efforts to save labor.

The primary incentive to innovation was economy of labor—the big item with a rising price. In the early 1900s wood was a large item, and its price was rising faster than that of most other inputs. But by the 1930s wood had become a less important factor of production. Because so much labor was expended in renewing or replacing worn-out and defective materials, however, one way to save labor was to make materials last longer. Innovation with the purpose of saving labor tended, therefore, to produce economies of materials as well. Since 1940 maintenance of way expenditures on the railroads have been restrained. They have risen less than total operating expenses. Outlays on ties and rails have risen still less, despite price increases—an indication of greater efficiency. Since 1947 even the outlays on track labor have been successfully restrained in spite of rising unit price. The research and innovation required to save labor seem to have produced payoffs or economies of every other input as well.

The same thing was happening in the sawmills, concentration yards (tie-contracting operations), and wood-preserving plants as on the railroads. Wage pressure was felt as early as the 1930s, and during the war there were great demands for wood, there were price restrictions, and there were shortages of labor and materials. Both the Wages and Hours Division and later the Office of Price Administration required new, more elaborate accounts. The "squeeze" forced mills and contractors to mechanize and to increase labor productivity. Lifts, hoists, cranes, moving belts, and other machinery were introduced. Gangs of tie handlers at wood-preserving plants and the yards were virtually eliminated. A "testimonial" from a large crosstie producer gives some indication of the value of the squeeze to productivity and efficiency of the industry: "If the experience of NRA and OPA accomplished nothing else, it must be said that the crosstie industry surely improved their appreciation and understanding of timber values, production cost and accounting, distribution and the end value of crossties." [17] His view is reminiscent of the restrictions of World War I, out of which "we discovered good things and we want to keep them." [18]

It is difficult to analyze with the same perspective the most recent developments in railroad timber utilization. Further consolidation of lines will doubtless produce changes in the marketing geography and the preferences of individual systems for certain species. But in the substitution of species the basic flexibility has been gained, and each line adjusts to local, current advantages of supply convenient to its own lines.

The practice of selling ties as a ready-made, finished product rather than a special order item is likely to grow, as rail systems continue to use fewer ties and to get out of the wood-preserving business themselves. This form of marketing also depends on the progress of the recent "assay-type" or performance specification for treated wood products. Formerly specifications for wood preserving were operational definitions: the consumer specified a treating process rather than a quality of treated product to be purchased on inspection.

Research aimed at defense problems in World War II and the Korean War produced new opportunities. Railroads such as the Burlington are showing trends similar to those in the construction industry; they are, for example, using more plywood (in car construction) and more paper products (such as grain doors, the inner doors that seal carloads of grain). Experimentation continues with veneered wood for crossties and compression and plastic impregnation to harden the section under the tie plate. Recent research suggests that associated with the decay of wood from action of living organisms there is a process of corrosion of wood in contact with iron. Chemical industries and railroads are testing a variety of protective "goops" and pads.[19] As in other construction and engineering, concrete and reinforced concrete continue to make inroads as substitutes for timber. At least one American railroad has made concrete ties standard. They are used more extensively on the French and other foreign railways. The purely "technical" problems can be overcome; the choice is a matter of economics.

Experiments continue along many lines, and the benefits of each are not yet clear. It is reasonably certain, however, that in the 1970s, as in the 1890s and early 1900s, the railroad consumer will continue to develop flexibility and enlarge his choices of material and methods. In his purchases of materials, he will continue to specify greater reliability and uniform quality with respect to certain properties. It is probable that he will continue the trend apparent since the 1930s of valuing materials increasingly in terms of his own labor inputs. His use of forest products will hold steady or grow only to the extent that research permits greater control of their properties.

No Public Priority for Utilization

After World War II the time seemed ripe for a new utilization campaign. The Forest Service had been concerned during the war with efficient conversion (harvesting and manufacture of timber),[20] and project personnel saw much room for progress. As in World War I, the Forest Products Laboratory expanded operations: its personnel increased from 180 to 700 during World War II and fell back to 350 after the war. The research done at the laboratory had generated new techniques of modifying wood properties, and its directors pressed the idea that they could be applied in civilian industries.[21] As mentioned earlier, the postwar climate of large, diversified American industries favored product research in general, and rising prices for forest products encouraged its application in that market. Consumers' more rigorous standards created a demand for research on timber properties.

Foresters preoccupied with silviculture were also beginning to admit that they faced problems of markets and uses. They began to discuss, for example, the problems of too much hickory and beech. They realized that supplying wood was not the only problem in the forest economy; it was necessary to generate a demand for it. The Forest Service created a "Forest Utilization Service" whose purpose was industrial application of new methods to reduce the high costs of conversion. However, personnel allocated to this program were few, they were dispersed to the several forest experiment stations, and their role was severely limited.

The Department of Commerce sponsored certain limited efforts to develop wood uses and wood-using industries. They had two motives: to create opportunities in small business for returning veterans; and to provide employment and income opportunities in regions of economic stagnation, such as the Appalachian hardwood region. Under a grant from the Area

Redevelopment Administration of the Department of Commerce, the Forest Service opened a Forest Products Utilization and Marketing Laboratory in West Virginia (1964).

By creating the utilization service and the utilization laboratory and by calling several conferences of consumers (of hickory and beech), the Forest Service has recognized the existence of serious problems of utilization in the forest economy: labor costs, returns to labor, and value or service to consumers. But these problems have not received any strong priorities in the allocation of money, personnel, or publicity. There has been a shift of agency resources to recreational demands, but with respect to the timber economy, in preaching and in practice, the Forest Service continues to emphasize the theme of "sawtimber depletion." Except for the loss of the old zeal and sparkle, Forest Service timber policy today does not differ from that in the administration of Gifford Pinchot half a century ago. Wilson Compton in 1944 expressed the lumber manufacturer's view of depletion "conservation" policy:

In normal periods the basic American forestry problem is not one of scarcities, but of surpluses; not of "timber famine" but of forest abundance. The timber-famine publicity of the last half century was effective in stirring public interest in forest conservation but it has helped put the forest problem in a false national perspective. Timber and forests in the past have been an outstanding target of fear psychology and of scarcity propaganda, since a long and distinguished line of forest statisticians have periodically warned that the end of commercial forest operations in one region or another was just around the corner. Many Americans still have a lingering suspicion that we are on the verge of forest famine. This has failed to materialize, not so much by erroneous arithmetic as because our best technicians as well as most forest owners have known so little about the phenomenal rate of timber growth where nature is given a fair chance.

> . . . the sooner we stop treating forestry as a perpetual "emergency," the more progress we will make in forest conservation. Forestry should be a promise; not a threat. People do not grow or invest in things they are afraid of or are uncertain about. They invest in things they have faith in.[22]

Understanding between foresters and lumbermen has been difficult, but cooperation between foresters and consumers of wood products, such as the railroads, is a rather solid tradition in spite of their differences. The railroad consumer's experience confirms the picture of abundance, value, use, and promise. Unfortunately, railroad experience was not promptly assimilated by the Forest Service.

The Myth and the Moral

The experience of the railroads as consumers of forest products provides a window on the American forest economy and puts the old predictions of timber famine and commercial disaster into a new perspective. The crucial error lay in an important confusion: physical facts of production and consumption were confused with economic facts of supply and demand. As everyone admitted in the early 1900s, it was not possible for the nation to continue indefinitely to consume more timber than it was producing. Some adjustment had to be made in the physical facts. There was considerable error in underestimating physical production, especially timber growth rates in the South and Northwest, and there was confusion about what kinds of growth should be counted. The basic material equation did, however, have to be adjusted in some way.

But from that observation the conservationists concluded that there would be certain grave economic consequences. They completely ignored the complex factors that constitute economic supply and economic demand and the relationship between them. The economic facts of supply, for example, were very different from the physical facts of supply. The physical supply of timber was diminishing, as everyone could see, but the economic supply probably was not. Careful distinction between physical and economic supply is essential in explaining the disagreement as to whether growing more wood (increasing physical supply) was the most practical and economical means of adjusting the material balance.

The economic facts of demand are subject to change over a period of years. Habits of consumption cannot be treated as "requirements" whose modification is likely to disrupt the economy. It was by adjusting their own purchasing behavior that railroad consumers contributed most to the long-run solution. Most economic theory deals with short-run analysis of supply and demand and was not helpful in predicting the long-run balance. In the long run, supply and demand curves were not independent.

Because both the supply and demand sides of the economic equation changed over the years, in ways very different from what was predicted for them in 1900, it is evident today that the American forest was in no real danger of disappearing under the rails, down the mine shafts, or up in smoke, and the "timber famine" was largely a myth.

These two crucial aspects—supply and demand for railway timber—are analyzed below. The role of the industrial consumer and the role of the public resource management agency are reviewed. Then the conclusions are summarized in a much more general form, in order to emphasize the points of comparison with current issues of management of other natural resources.

Chapter 9

Expansion of Economic Supply

In an economic sense, supply is a function relating price to quantity offered for sale. The supply of timber is not really a single function, and it is misleading to treat timber supply as an abstract homogeneous resource. Probably the three most important differentiating factors are the location of the timber, the size of the trees (related to their age), and the differences of species. The three are interrelated to some degree, and they are meaningful only in terms of intended uses and markets for the timber.

Location of timber relative to location of demand, for example, produces great variation in the delivered cost to the consumer. The size of the tree affects substantially the costs of harvesting and manufacturing. Woods of various species have a wide range of properties, and even the wood of a single selected tree is extremely variable material. The utility of wood in general and of each particular species lies in our ability to take advantage of its several properties. The nature of the final product must be specified in order to determine fully the relevant supply function. For example, in some uses wood is valued for its durability or resistance to acids or living organisms, and for other uses durability can be ignored. In some uses timbers are valued for their hardness, or for the great size or uniformity of the piece. Consequently the character of use affects the degree to which various species or pieces of wood can be substituted for one another. The end use affects the costs of processing the raw timber—seasoning, chemical treatment, sorting, and handling—and, therefore, the price-quantity relation.

Certain factors in the adjustment that took place in the supply of forest products to the railroads were the result of outside developments in parts of the economy other than forestry and railroading. They did not affect the physical supply of timber, but they constituted a revolution in terms of the economic supply. There was no disastrous timber shortage partly because the factors that tended to reduce the supply available at a given price were outweighed by other factors that tended to make more timber available at that price.

The most important of these factors was the dramatic improvement in access to timber. Railroads tapped one new region after another and from the 1870s linked them together in a flexible system. Specialized logging railroads opened up localities not commercially accessible earlier. After World War I the use of trucks and the construction of roads halved the cost of hauling timber and thus increased the amount of timber that could be offered at a given price. It may well be true that the United States had 820,000,000 acres of forests in 1800 and only 495,000,000 in 1933, or 509,000,000 commercial acres in 1963,[1] but these figures are wholly irrelevant to the economic facts of supply. Today the nation has a much larger acreage of timberland accessible at the same real cost than it had in 1800 or in 1900.

Progress in the technology of harvesting timber products has also contributed to the expansion of supply. Mechanization and economies of scale have made it possible for very large sawmills to supply timber over long distances to eastern cities. Increased efficiency of very small (portable) mills has made it possible to market timber from rugged topography and small woodlots throughout the zones of demand.

Since World War I progressive agricultural technology has improved the productivity of farmland, so that more and more agricultural land has returned to forest, and little forest-land has been cleared for agriculture. This contradicts the expectations of the early 1900s, based on observed trends of increasing population and land in farms. The groundwork of new agricultural technology had been laid by 1910, but, as in the field of transport, its impact was not yet evident.

Mechanization of agriculture has also given greater value to flatland and made rugged and inaccessible areas less attractive for farming. Indeed, the gasoline engine and tractor, the very inventions that made it cheaper to exploit remote highlands for timber, also reduced their value for farming. The timber management alternative became somewhat more attractive. It might be more accurate to say that, as other uses were abandoned, timber took over.

If factors other than physical supply affected the economics of timber supply, it also follows that efforts to expand physical supply of standing timber were not necessarily the best way to meet a problem of economic adjustment. It has been recognized for centuries that the physical supply of timber cannot be expanded easily or quickly. The railroads' experiments with growing timber added new evidence that silviculture was no solution. In the early 1900s the railroads tried "growing their own" and decided that it was not the economic answer to the timber user's problems. Scientific methods of fire control, seeding, and logging might contribute to protection of forest and watershed investments, but there were no real shortcuts to producing timber or reducing the amount of long-term capital required. Forestry under the economic conditions of the early 1900s and the foreseeable future was not attractive "in the light of money-making." It was least attractive to an industry that had more rewarding alternative uses for its capital, and more rewarding technical alternatives for controlling its outlays on timber. Seen in isolation, forestry appeared to be a reasonable proposition, as federal foresters argued,[2] but the railroad men looked at it in a broader economic framework—as one of a number of choices open to them, but by no means the most attractive one.

The railroad experiments made it clear by 1915 that forest management was economically justified only where land was worthless or the holding of land could be justified on other grounds. Wherever there were alternative uses—agricultural, industrial, residential, commercial—which gave value to the land, forestry could not compete. Since access to markets was a major factor in opening up alternatives, most land along the railroads, unless it was being held for speculation, future development, or water management, was not suited for forestry. Forestry was best suited to the most remote and least accessible lands of the nation. Related to this was acceptance of the least intensive practices of forest management, that is, using the smallest possible amounts of other factors of production—labor and management—over the long term. The railroads found these principles of forestry appropriate in the American economy, in strong contrast to European examples of forestry. Again, the railroad men saw forest location and production methods in the broad framework of economic alternatives. After World War I the tie producers of Missouri and Tennessee, through their own experience, largely unplanned, rediscovered the same principles. Their pragmatic forestry depended on minimum input of labor, land of low value, and exceptionally cheap transport.

Changing Character of Economic Demand

Over the years the pattern of economic demand also changed radically. Demand is a function relating price to quantity that consumers will buy. New technology again explains the changes, but here the new techniques were generated inside the railroad and forest products industries. They arose mainly from consumer responses to threats or experiences of price changes.

Demand changed in the direction of much lower average consumption of timber by railroads and a greater flexibility or broader set of technical alternatives. The railroad consumer today spends more of his forest products dollar for processing and modification of the properties of the wood product and less for the raw material. He is more sensitive to added costs of labor related to the use of the material than he is to the cost of the raw material itself.

The technological developments that made possible the new market behavior were remarkably diverse in their technical means: chemical preserving of wood, new engineering design, patented protective devices such as tie plates and fasteners, standards to control quality of materials purchased, and considerable substitution of one material for another—timber, plywood, and paper, concrete, steel, light metals, and plastics. The several techniques frequently offered sets of alternatives. For example, wood preserving and redesign of timber bridges and their joints offered one solution to the problem of higher-cost bridge timber. The development of concrete piling and steel bridges offered alternatives. Research on several fronts was complementary, and each new solution added to the consumer's flexibility and his ability to meet the ever changing market conditions for his several inputs.

In all the technical fields, but above all in wood preserving, railroad consumers made important research contributions. Examples are reviewed here to illustrate the various ways in which innovation occurred as a mechanism of response to economic incentives.

In the 1880s the railroads studied and rationalized wood-preserving know-how in response to a fear of timber famine (Chapter 4). Later they developed industrial standards of wood preserving in response to changes in the price of wood (Chapter 6). It is important to notice that decisive responses were made to modest changes or even threats; they did not wait for "disaster." It is also important to underline the fact that the railroads realized economies that more than compensated for the higher price of wood. There appears to have been a net increase in the efficiency of the entire maintenance of way program each time an improvement was made to restrain a particular cost. For example, labor savings were at first a by-product of making wood last longer, as its price rose. Now further economies of timber and steel are realized through efforts to save labor (Chapter 8).

Some improvements that saved money and reduced demand for wood were initiated by changes in the railroads' or their suppliers' business organization. The most dramatic were new purchasing and accounting practices that resulted from railroad consolidation in the 1880s, the organization of technical and professional associations in the early 1900s, and successive waves of government regulation of interstate commerce, wages and hours, and wartime prices. Each reorganization and regulation required new methods of keeping records and accounts, which in turn allowed managers to analyze their operations and thus recognize problems worth study and change.

In the late 1800s, for example, the Burlington made an inspection and inventory of all storehouses on its newly acquired lines in order to make their practices uniform. The effort to simplify and standardize specifications and control inventories produced substantial economies in the purchase of timber and metal items, in addition to the economies of buying on a larger scale.

Wages and hours laws (1934) and the wage and price controls during World War II had similar effects on cross-tie producers and other lumbermills. The small mill operators subjected to wage controls discovered, for example, that labor costs were more important to them than any other costs, and they could save labor by simple changes such as stocking spare parts and maintaining equipment. They also discovered they could save by selecting the larger trees. The Forest Service had been urging this practice for forty years, on grounds of efficient timber growth, but mills did not accept the idea until they discovered that it meant profit for them through labor savings.

Some technical changes arose, as shown, from the effort to solve a well-defined problem, usually to control the rising price of some factor relative to others. Other technical changes occurred as a result of the fortuitous appearance of a problem and a perceived opportunity; that was the pattern in the substitution of one species of timber for another. The successive introductions of chestnut oak for crossties and short-leaf yellow pines for bridge timber (1890s), treated red oak for ties (about 1910), then Doublas fir, mixed hardwoods (1920s), the gums (1940s), and hickory (1950s), each required some research and some modification of handling, seasoning, treating, and utilization. The research that made these species substitutions possible was done through a combination of circumstances. The prices of the best-known eastern timbers—white oak, longleaf pine, white pine, cypress—rose as physical and economic supply were reduced. This posed a problem for the consumer. At the same time the extension of railroads and settlement opened up new timber regions of species unknown in eastern markets, and the remaining eastern stands still contained large amounts of timber whose value was low because their properties were unknown or misunderstood. Thus opportunities were ripe. Douglas fir is an interesting case because, in addition to the pressure of high prices for other species and the new low-cost opportunity of exploiting the very large Douglas fir timber, railroads were nonetheless reluctant to adopt it for crossties until they were literally forced to do so. The U.S. Railroad Administration required its acceptance in order to reduce freight car movements in the period 1918–1919. The same combination of pressures was necessary to induce railroads to agree on a standard specification for crossties (Chapter 7).

Many of the pressures that induced changes in the habits of

consumers and suppliers or induced research with substantial payoffs were unwelcome. The various bureaucratic controls and accounts were, and still are, vigorously protested. But unwelcome pressures frequently produced long-run gains in efficiency. The dramatic reorganizations that were required in times of war and in the 1930s produced dramatic technical progress in railroad maintenance of way as in other industries.

Jacob Schmookler has pointed out that the numerous small improvements of an invention over the years have tended to contribute more to rising productivity than the single important invention of a given moment.[3] This is undoubtedly true of railroad maintenance of way. The organization of the railroads and their suppliers for research and communication of technical ideas has been vital to that process of continual improvement. For example, the testing, research, and purchasing methods established by the large railroads in the period of transition from iron to steel rail (1870s) were subsequently applied to timber and other materials (Chapter 4).

Industry-wide associations of engineers, purchasing agents, and wood preservers made numerous contributions. While they cannot be strictly classified, they seem to have functioned more effectively as consumer organizations than as producer organizations. Although they were institutions for sharing information and setting uniform standards—specific kinds of collusion—their performance contributed substantially to competition and increasing efficiency both in the railroad industry and its supplier industries.

The railroads and other industrial consumers of timber may also take substantial credit for maintaining effective demand for public research in wood technology for seventy-five years. The Forest Products Laboratory, administered by the Forest Service, was created and defended through the efforts of consumers. Its work has been supported to a large extent by their cooperative funds, and its later expansions occurred through wartime public defense grants—another large industrial consumer (Chapter 7).

Investment in research was a major problem-solving tool of industry. Research took place in order to solve recognized problems. The rising cost of some specific factor of production is the sort of problem that was most quickly recognized in industry. Therefore, when factors outside the industrial consumer's control increased the price of an input, industrial research was mobilized to shift the demand function for that input. In railroad maintenance of way this adjustment took a period of some years. It was longer than the business cycle apparently because the industry had to recognize a noncyclical trend in order to identify the problem. The lag for technical research seems to have been small but variable, and there was more often a substantial lag in the rate at which the innovation could be made to pay off. In wood preserving, for example, critical research took place in the 1880s in response to problems of local shortages, which were in fact solved by other means (hauling, species substitutions, and so forth), and the technology of wood preserving was thus sketched well before wood prices rose generally and before it became economical to practice wood preserving. Once a definite problem of price trend was recognized, wood-preserving techniques were adopted swiftly. In 1907–1908, for example, the Burlington adopted a set of innovations for which the payoffs rose gradually for twenty years and were still substantial after twenty-five or thirty years, when further innovations (the new standard of 1931) began to yield returns.

Focus on physical volumes produced and consumed led inevitably to alarm as long as the amount of standing timber in the country was declining, or believed to be declining. Even today, focus on physical volumes fosters concern about the depletion of certain types of material—our "large sawlogs," our "virgin timber," or selected species such as walnut, redwood, or Douglas fir. Contemporary official forestry policy is a material balance or equation of physical units of timber grown and required annually, without relation to price. This is the theory known as sustained yield.

Focus on physical productivity also led inevitably to pre-occupation with silviculture. If "needs" or quantity "requirements" were fixed at levels above what was being produced, the only solution was to grow more wood. The railroad story has shown clearly that reduction of "requirements" did more to restore balance than silvicultural schemes. Over the long run (fifty years) and the short run (five to ten years), modifying use proved to be a cheaper and swifter approach to solving the problem of the scarcity of resources than trying to modify nature's complex system of supply.

In their concern with silviculture, American foresters tended to rely on European examples as their model. Here, too, the dependence on physical measures of productivity encouraged unrealistic or uneconomic goals. Annual growth or physical yields of American forests of the Southeast and Northwest are greater than most European forests because of climates, but if allowance is made for the climatic advantage, American yields are relatively low. In Europe labor is lavished on the forests. But, as the railroads found, in the American economy of higher labor values and lower timber values, it was uneconomical to use European methods to increase physical output.

In line with European methods and the internal logic of the "material balance" approach, the Forest Service uses the sustained yield principle as a guide to local year-to-year forest management as well as overall long-run national planning. On all working circles or small regional units of forest under its management, the agency attempts to apply sustained yield or obtain an equation of annual growth and annual harvest.[4] The physical equation ignores the price of land or value of location as well as other variables that affect the price of wood from year to year. This does not necessarily produce the most economical pattern of land use in view of the great variation of competing uses, forest productivity, and costs of transport between regions. The Forest Service has traditionally considered long hauls of timber to be a wasteful and expensive threat. Consumers, however, as we have seen, frequently preferred this type of substitution, as new know-how made transport cheaper. In the same way the application of the physical equation on a year-to-year short-run basis is inconsistent with economic efficiency.

A choice of physical measures of "waste" rather than economic measures has also tended to slant research and control efforts in directions that are not economic. The Forest Service has, for example, advertised widely the large volume of waste in treetops, branches, stumps, sawdust, and scrap left from harvest, manufacture, and fabrication of wood products. The Forest Products Laboratory has sought uses for sawdust, but its success has been modest if measured in terms of values rather than volumes recovered. (Better machinery to produce less sawdust has proved more valuable through savings to the manufacturer.) The kinds of waste that interested manufacturers and consumers, as shown by the National Committee on Wood Utilization (Chapter 7), were demonstrable in dollars and cents, not in cubic feet of unmarketable materials.

Because of its preoccupation with physical quantities of growth and drain, the Forest Service sometimes proposed conservation practices that were uneconomical. For example, it advised tie producers to take larger trees for crossties and let the small ones grow, in order to maximize rates of growth of timber, but at the same time it urged the railroads to use smaller ties, in order to reduce drain. This was uneconomical from the manufacturer's point of view because it wasted labor and raised the price. It was uneconomical from the railroad engineer's point of view because the smaller tie would not stand up as long, and the annual cost would increase. From the point of view of conservation in the long run, it was questionable: more smaller ties would be required, and more smaller trees would be cut to meet the need (Chapters 6 and 7). Obviously the advice of the Forest Service was not followed, and to that degree its "natural position as adviser in all forest matters" was compromised.

The most serious consequence of alarmism based on material equations of growth and drain was probably the bias it introduced into the consumer's own research. The Forest Service, to reduce drain of recurrent large-volume uses, urged the substitution of metal and concrete, as in crossties and bridges. The patriot used "permanent materials" wherever possible. The consequence of the constant pressure to develop substitutes was a long, gradual devaluation of wood, arrested perhaps since World War II. Certainly the Forest Service does not bear the sole responsibility, but it did influence the research decisions of consumers at a critical time. Alarmism and urging of substitutions also tended to demoralize the lumber manufacturers. Their pessimistic view of future markets was one reason for their lack of research. Until World War II they were among the slowest industries to mechanize, improve quality control, or seek new ways to manipulate the properties of their materials.

Since the administration of Gifford Pinchot, beginning in 1898, the primary interest of the Forest Service has been silviculture, a small segment of the whole forest economy. The consumer has directly or indirectly generated most of the progress in the economic use of wood and value added to wood, while the Forest Service was oriented toward European ideals of twig gathering in forest management and sawdust economies in wood utilization.

The role of Pinchot must therefore be appraised more critically than it has been by historians of conservation. Certainly Pinchot made a unique contribution to public awareness of natural resources, especially forest resources. But the commitment of his agency to "Forestry in the Woods" has limited its capacity to analyze and think creatively about the nation's total forest problem. Although Pinchot is generally credited with expanding the nation's thinking about the timber economy, he appears in the above view to have narrowed it. He introduced a high degree of professionalism in forestry and put strong emphasis on silviculture in the education of foresters. But the wholly admirable professional standards and silvicultural bias of forestry education have been a straitjacket on the Forest Service, by their overemphasis on physical forestry rather than economics, on supply rather than demand, and on efficient growth of wood rather than its efficient use and service.

As it looks from the railway timber story, the men who made great contributions to forest values and forest products research stand in contrast to Pinchot. Wilson Compton, Hermann von Schrenk, Ernest Sterling, and Bernhard Fernow were men whose education and experience were broad and whose view of the forest economy extended from seedling through service life of the wood product. Fernow in particular, Pinchot's immediate predecessor, considered timber physics or research on the use of wood as "the pivotal science of the art of forestry." As an agency, the Department of Commerce made a significant and largely unrecognized contribution to forestry as the sponsor of standards and technical research. Like the individuals mentioned, that department pressed for a broader view of the forest economy and for cooperation among producers, protection agencies, manufacturers, and consumers. It tended to use the consumer as the catalyst.

Observations on Resource Management

Some limited generalizations can be drawn from railway timber history that raise serious questions for the management of other natural resources today.

Throughout this story we have set aside the aesthetic, ethical, and human values which we may want to attach to our forests, our wilderness, our farm life, or our system of ownership or social organization. They are important matters, perhaps decisive to resource management policy, but are less susceptible to economic analysis. Railroad purchases offer no insight into such matters.

Many national inquiries into natural resources concentrate primarily on the issues of efficient future operation of our present economic system.[5] To that extent, resource management is and must be concerned with the economics of supply and demand. It is in this area that railroad purchasing is a relevant example. The railway timber story demonstrates clearly that material balances or trends and equations of physical production and consumption are not an adequate basis for predicting the nature of the economic adjustments to be expected. Planning for the allocation and management of resources requires that we pay attention to all the factors that enter into economic supply and demand. Many studies have been and still are devoted mainly to the physical bases of supply, to the neglect of the economics of supply, and to the greater neglect of demand.

When attention is focused too narrowly on the physical basis of supply, there is a tendency, as in the case of timber, to treat the resource as a distinct homogeneous substance, measurable in cubic feet or tons. But the railroads found that species differences permitted a high degree of technical substitution and thus increased the opportunities of supply. Variations in their properties allowed their modification and more efficient use, and therefore substantial reductions in total demand. The same diversity of technical alternatives or opportunities can be found in soil or water today. For example, seawater, brackish water, effluents of sewage treatment plants, mineralized groundwaters of various temperature ranges, purified municipal supplies, and distilled water have quite different properties and values for a great variety of uses, and the costs of modifying them or substituting one for another vary greatly. Yet in general discussion of water shortages and engineering solutions, the complex characteristics of economic demand for water were systematically ignored until the 1960s.[6]

In their purchases and their experiments with growing their own timber, the railroads acknowledged the importance of location and the spatial structure of the supply and demand for timber and the land on which it grew, and the costs of transport. Yet in planning for soil conservation and grandiose reclamation projects in recent years, we have continued to ignore the spatial structure of markets for land and for the products of the soil.

As the railway timber story shows, the great difficulty in predicting demand and part of the difficulty in predicting economic changes in supply lie in predicting technological change. It is extremely difficult to predict rates of progress in transport and mechanization and their impact on a specific resource and industry.[7] The foresters cannot be expected to have foreseen in 1908 the future role of the gasoline engine in cutting costs of logging and lumbering, or as a limitation on the flourishing railroad industry. But some types of technology, we have seen, were generated within the consumer and processor industries in order to compensate for expected price changes of various factors. That particular type of technical change should be studied more carefully. The various substitutions, as of concrete, steel, and among wood products, are susceptible to economic analysis and to a degree of prediction.

What is more important, those changes are subject to a degree of control. It is widely agreed that the various natural resources have the same basic limitation as timber—their physical supply cannot be easily expanded, and their economic supply is inelastic as compared with other products. Then it is important to generate new technology, with emphasis on means of using the resource more efficiently.

A growing demand for a resource appears to be healthy and conducive to increasing efficiency of use and high levels of research and investment to reduce costs of extraction, processing, and shipping,[8] that is, techniques that shift the supply curve down and compensate for the effects of physical "depletion" on price. It is more important still, from the point of view of consumers, to generate the technology that will permit increasing flexibility, or an ever broader range of substitution of materials, methods, and sources of supply. An economy of growth is necessarily one of continual change, and flexibility must be built in through technology as well as organization, for swift adaptation and adjustment with minimal disruption.

It is not obvious just what kind of public organization can produce such breadth in resource management planning and research. The timber story suggests that a crusade may not be the best foundation and that compartmentalization may be a handicap. One agency (public) was charged with protecting the physical supply of the timber resource; others (private) were charged with its extraction and processing; still others (both public and private) were the consumers. Planning and research on the forest products economy as a whole were in no-man's-land. The Department of Commerce seems in the 1920s to have successfully forged constructive policies and standards from the conflicts of viewpoint (Chapter 7). But that kind of organization, with conflicts internalized, was of delicate balance and limited enforcement power, and it did not survive.

Specific agencies charged with materials and engineering

research—the Bureau of Standards, for example—made contributions to the forest products economy. The Forest Service itself was strikingly creative during that early period as the Division of Forestry, when its charge from Congress, its tiny budget, and its director, Fernow, limited it to functioning as a research agency with almost no powers of management or administration. In the early 1900s, as the Bureau of Forestry, its products laboratories, relatively independent and located in agricultural and engineering schools, were also successful in generating the kinds of technology of use that have been urged here. Since 1910 the central Forest Products Laboratory has achieved some of its greatest success through financing and direction of contracts for the defense consumer, not the Forest Service.

The example of the railroads suggests that industrial consumers of resources have a contribution to make to good resource management and that what counts is the degree to which they are organized for scientific analysis and marketing pressure. But it must be recognized that the buyer for the railroad paid a market price for his timber. This case differs from that of industries that use streams or atmosphere for waste discharge or abandon strip-mined land. Unless an industry pays a price that reflects changing conditions of supply and demand, it will not respond to changes or attempt to "economize" through new research or the application of known techniques. Agencies for public resource management will have to find ways to take advantage of the market incentives and structures that can induce "economizing" research. Research is the chief tool for increasing the productivity, value, and substitutability of resources.

"Conservation" should mean continually increasing our opportunities and our flexibility in the use and substitution of many resources for many kinds of satisfactions. This interpretation implies moral issues since the dollar does not measure all kinds of satisfactions for all individuals equally well. But this interpretation also suggests, in the light of the railway timber experience, that the consumers—the people to be satisfied—must continually work to clarify the nature of their demand. The services and functions to be performed by a given "resource" are continually changing, and the relative values of these services are constantly shifting. The public agencies traditionally charged with ensuring the wise use of resources must be aware of the eventual services, functions, or end uses to which a resource is put and sensitive to the impact of new know-how on values or "demands."

The Role of the Forest Service

The conclusions above are based primarily on a study made from the timber consumer's records and point of view. But they raise certain questions about the role of the Forest Service. Like many younger resource management agencies, the Forest Service was created to deal with a crisis—the imminent depletion of the nation's forest resource. Since 1898 it has been committed to growing more wood as a basic remedy. As shown above, major industrial consumers of wood have preferred other solutions and seem not to have suffered from "depletion."

In recent years the Forest Service has gradually turned its attention to other uses and values of the forests, especially recreation. But in looking at problems of timber growth and harvest, the agency has continued to "view with alarm." The explanation seems to lie in the persistent habit of thinking in terms of physical or material quantities instead of economic values. This methodological habit has perpetuated a strong bias in the agency's interpretations of the past, its expectations of the future, and its management and research policies.

The concept of multiple use of forests, introduced early by

Pinchot, was popularized during the New Deal and has become ever more important in all federal land management and resource investment decisions. The growing emphasis on multiple use is promising because it requires analyses in terms of values (costs and benefits). The uses of a forested area for various forms of recreation and for timber production, for example, cannot be added together or compared as conflicting alternatives, as long as we talk about cubic feet of timber and numbers of hunters, skiers, campers, boaters, or motorists. They must be compared in terms of value measures: jobs, income produced, dollars spent, or votes. The growing efforts of the Forest Service to measure and compare values of diverse uses of the forests have already introduced more sophisticated economic and operations research and a broader framework of thinking. It will doubtless produce more realistic evaluations of the timber economy than in the past.

Notes and Index

Notes

Chapter 1

1. Theodore Roosevelt, "The Forest in the Life of a Nation," *Proceedings of the American Forest Congress held at Washington, D.C., January 2 to 6, 1905,* under the auspices of the American Forestry Association (Washington, D.C.: Suter, 1905), 8; also reprinted in "What Forestry Means to Representative Men," U.S. Department of Agriculture, Bureau of Forestry, *Circular* (No. 33, 1905), 9.

Chapter 2

1. The Central Pacific, in addition to the usual ties, 2,640 to the mile, and immense quantities of bridge timber, used wood fuel during the construction period, built 6,213 feet of tunnels in the Sierra Nevada, all lined with wood, and in 1867–1869 erected 37 miles of snowsheds and snow galleries which required 65,000,000 board feet of lumber and 900 tons of iron and cost over $2,000,000. Wood trestles were as high as 90 feet, as long as 400 feet, and had as much as a mile of structural "approach." A telegraph line along the track required timber. The Union Pacific built 25 miles of snow fences and 4 miles of snowsheds before 1873. John Debo Galloway, *The First Transcontinental Railroad, Central Pacific-Union Pacific* (New York: Simmons-Boardman, 1950).

2. The expression is that of Howard Miller, general agent of the Union Pacific Railroad, in *The Forester,* III (Jan. 1, 1897), 6. He referred to locomotive fires as well as consumption. Lumber required for car construction and repair is harder to estimate, but tended to increase until about 1910. In 1918 it amounted to at least another two billion board feet a year.

3. Bernhard Fernow asserted that monopsony and the seasonal surplus of farm labor were factors restraining the price of ties in the 1880s. "Although [the prices of] lumber and dimension stock

are on the ascendancy, the value of ties is comparatively stationary, lower even today in certain sections than 10 or 15 years ago . . . The railroads have full control in the selection of the best quality and the price paid, while by a regulation of the rates of freight they can prevent an undue export . . . In this way prices are kept down. Immense quantities are delivered at prices below its real value." "Report on the Relation of Railroads to Forest Supplies and Forestry," U.S. Department of Agriculture, Division of Forestry, *Bulletin* (No. 1, 1887), 13.

4. Timber agents reported over a period of several years that they could not protect Illinois Central lands against timber thieves. Some of the applicants for land made down payments on IC land-grant property, then stripped the area of timber and abandoned the land. Juries in the area were not partial to the railroad, and on at least one occasion convicted the railroad agent for confiscating ties cut off railroad land by a gang of timber thieves. Paul W. Gates, *The Illinois Central Railroad and Its Colonization Work* (Cambridge, Mass.: Harvard University Press, 1934), 324–329.

5. Depredations and abuses are described extensively in the reports of Franklin B. Hough, especially U.S. Department of Agriculture, *Report upon Forestry*, II, prepared by Franklin B. Hough (Washington, D.C.: Government Printing Office, 1880), 16. Before 1879 cases were reported from Alabama (Mobile and Girard Railroad Company); Sabine River, Louisiana; the Canadian Pacific Railroad; Osage River, Missouri, where half a million ties were stolen; and French and Brush Creeks, Wyoming. See also *Report of the Committee appointed by the National Academy of Sciences upon the inauguration of a forest policy for the forested lands of the U.S. to the Secretary of the Interior* (Washington, D.C., 1897).

6. For the survey of 1877, see U.S. Department of Agriculture, *Report upon Forestry*, I, prepared by Franklin B. Hough (Washington, D.C.: Government Printing Office, 1878), 112–118. For a more extended survey of 1882, see F. B. Hough, "Report on Kinds and Quantities of Timber Used for Railroad Ties," in U.S. Department of Agriculture, *Report on Forestry*, IV, prepared by N. H. Egleston (Washington, D.C.: Government Printing Office, 1884), 119–173.

Chapter 3

1. Perry Miller, *Errand into the Wilderness* (Cambridge, Mass.: Belknap Press of Harvard University Press, 1956).

2. See *Garden and Forest, Forestry and Irrigation, American Forestry.*

3. John Evelyn, *Sylva, or A Discourse of forest-trees, and the propagation of timber in His Majesties Dominions* (London, 1664).

4. John U. Nef, *The Rise of the British Coal Industry* (London: Routledge, 1932); Archibald and Nan Clow, *The Chemical Revolution, A Contribution to Social Technology* (London: Batchwork Press, 1952). The opposing view is argued by Michael W. Flinn, "Timber and the Advance of Technology, A Reconsideration," *Annals of Science,* XV (No. 2, 1959), 108.

5. John A. Warder, "Report on Forests and Forestry," in U.S. Commission to the Vienna Exhibition, 1873, *Reports,* I (Washington, D.C., 1875–1876); and George Perkins Marsh, *Man and Nature* (New York, 1864).

6. Andrew S. Fuller, *Forest Tree Culturist: A Treatise on the Cultivation of American Forest Trees* (New York, 1866).

7. It is, in fact, a reason for the absence of forests. See the discussion by Ashley L. Schiff, *Fire and Water, Scientific Heresy in the Forest Service* (Cambridge, Mass.: Harvard University Press, 1962).

8. D. C. Burson, "Forest Tree Planting as an Investment," *Proceedings of American Forestry Congress 1883 at St. Paul* (Washington, D.C., 1884), 18–20.

9. Richard C. Overton, *Burlington West, A Colonization History of the Burlington Railroad* (Cambridge, Mass.: Harvard University Press, 1941). Overton discusses the Burlington and Missouri River Railroad settlement ventures. Information on the plantations is found in the Tree Papers, MS. 63 1870 8.13, Burlington Archives, Newberry Library, Chicago.

10. See William L. Hall and Hermann von Schrenk, "The Hardy Catalpa," U.S. Department of Agriculture, Forest Service, *Bulletin* (No. 37, 1902); and John P. Brown, *Practical Arboriculture* (Connersville, Ind., 1906).

11. Leonard B. Hodges, *Forest Tree Planter's Manual* (3d ed., Minneapolis, 1883).

12. U.S. Department of Agriculture, *Report upon Forestry,* I, prepared by Franklin B. Hough (Washington, D.C.: Government Printing Office, 1878), 26.

13. The Boston forest congress in 1885 discussed spark arresters for locomotives. Hough's successor, Egleston, was most interested in fire control. His reports as Forester were largely devoted to this problem. He estimated that railroads were the third principal cause of forest fires and were responsible in 1880 for 13 percent of fires and damage. See "Report on the Relation of Railroads to Forest Supplies and Forestry," U.S. Department of Agriculture, Division of Forestry, *Bulletin* (No. 1, 1887), Appendix 4 (prepared by N. H. Egleston), 128.

14. B. E. Fernow, *Report upon the Forestry Investigations of the U.S. Department of Agriculture, 1877–1898,* 55 Cong., 3 sess., 1899, House Doc. 181, 22.

15. B. E. Fernow, address, *Forestry Quarterly,* I (Jan. 1902), 42.

Chapter 4

1. Similar problems and reforms occurred with respect to castings, fuel, and other items. Timber products are used here as examples.

2. Peter Temin has described the importance of the demand for rail in the progress of ferrous metallurgy; see his *Iron and Steel in Nineteenth-Century America, An Economic Inquiry* (Cambridge, Mass.: M.I.T. Press, 1964).

3. Paul H. Dudley, "Structure of Certain Timber-Ties, Behavior and Cause of the Decay," U.S. Department of Agriculture, Division of Forestry, *Bulletin* (No. 1, 1887), Appendix 1, 31–65.

4. J. B. Johnson, *The Materials of Construction* (4th ed., New York: John Wiley, 1914). For economic relations, see pp. 606–612, tables and graphs.

5. Temin, *Iron and Steel,* describes a similar stimulus to metallurgical technology arising from changes in access to bodies of ore and changing types of demand in various geographical regions.

6. "The Woods of the United States," *Report on the Forests of North America (exclusive of Mexico)*, 47 Cong., 2 sess., 1884, House Misc. Doc. 42, Pt. IX, 247–481.

7. "Timber Physics," U.S. Department of Agriculture, Division of Forestry, *Bulletin* (No. 6, Pt. I, 1892).

8. B. E. Fernow, *Report upon the Forestry Investigations of the U.S. Department of Agriculture, 1877–1898*, 55 Cong., 3 sess., 1899, House Doc. 181, 22.

9. E. E. Russell Tratman, "Preliminary Report on the Use of Metal Track on Railways as Substitutes for Wooden Ties," U.S. Department of Agriculture, Division of Forestry, *Bulletin* (No. 3, 1889).

10. B. E. Fernow, *Some Peculiarities of Wood*, Address to 32nd Annual Convention of American Institute of Architects, Washington, D.C., Nov. 2, 1898 (Washington, D.C., 1899).

11. *Report of a Committee of the American International Association of Railway Superintendents of Bridges and Buildings on Strength of Bridge and Trestle Timbers*, reprinted in A. L. Johnson, "Economical Designing of Timber Trestle Bridges," U.S. Department of Agriculture, Division of Forestry, *Bulletin* (No. 12, 1896), 41–57.

12. U.S. Department of Agriculture, Division of Forestry, *Bulletin* (No. 12, 1896).

13. A few Kyanized chestnut ties were laid on the Northern Central Railroad near Baltimore in the 1830s, and the Kyan process was used on the canal locks at Lowell, Massachusetts, in 1848–1850 and after 1862. H. F. Weiss, *The Preservation of Structural Timber* (New York: McGraw-Hill, 1916).

14. The process used was Seeley's 1867 patent, which applied creosote in an open tank, without pressure. The technique depended on temperature changes to create conditions for penetration of the wood.

15. J. W. Putnam supervised work from 1875 at the Louisville and Nashville Railroad treating plant near New Orleans. In 1879 the New Orleans and Northeastern Railroad used creosote. In 1874 the Central Railroad of New Jersey built a pressure treating plant at Elizabethport, New Jersey, and in 1877 the Eppinger and Russell plant was built on Long Island to serve the Hudson River

Railroad. The Widener Library, Harvard University, contains numerous pamphlets describing the patented processes. The principal authorities who could be cited by commercial men at the time were those taking part in the 1850 discussions of the London Institute of Civil Engineers. The Hayford process called for steaming at 240° or 270° F. to season the wood, "coagulate the albumen," and render the wood "non-fermentable." The Bethell process restricted temperatures to 100° F. in order not to injure wood fibers. The Bethell process is still employed.

16. The Wellhouse process used zinc chloride, followed by a bath in a glue-tannin mixture that was supposed to coagulate the albumen, make it tough and leathery, and prevent the zinc compound from leaching out. The theory was absurd, but the treatment was reasonably effective in lengthening the service life of ties. A description and history of its use by the Atchison, Topeka, and Santa Fe Railroad is in Samuel M. Rowe, *Handbook of Timber Preservation* (Souvenir Ed., Chicago, 1904).

17. "Report on Wood Preservation," *Transactions,* American Society of Civil Engineers, XIV (1885), 247.

18. The ASCE report followed by one year the report of Samuel Boulton to the British Institute of Civil Engineers on the subject. See Samuel B. Boulton, *On the Antiseptic Treatment of Timber* (London, 1884). Statistical techniques of the Austrian railways of the 1870s were adopted. For example, a railroad could measure the proportion of ties removed each year from a lot of given date and treatment, and cumulative percentage curves for various lots could be compared.

19. "Report on Wood Preservation," 290.

20. *Ibid.,* 249.

21. Paul H. Dudley, comment on Hermann von Schrenk's and B. E. Fernow's papers, *Proceedings,* New York Railroad Club, XIII (Apr. 17, 1903), 212.

22. A. M. Wellington, comment on "Report on Wood Preservation," *Transactions,* American Society of Civil Engineers, XIV (1885), 394.

23. Charles Latimer, comment on "Report on Wood Preservation," *ibid.,* 396–397.

Chapter 5

1. Tie prices in Maine doubled for white cedar, 1902–1908. W. T. Osgood and B. L. Roberts, "Production of Railroad Ties in the State of Maine" (mimeo., Library of University of Maine, 1909). A Pennsylvania Railroad representative estimated that tie prices to the PRR rose three cents a year, 1899–1908. C. W. Tiffany, "Some Notes on Wood Preservation," address to foresters' convention, Harrisburg, in *Forest Leaves,* XIII (Aug. 1910), 154. On the Lake Shore and Michigan Southern and the Lake Erie and Western, white oak tie prices held steady from 1887 to 1896, but advanced 65 percent from 1897 to 1907. Lumber prices advanced 78 percent, railroad iron 53 percent, locomotive fuel 35 percent, and the average for all materials purchased by the railroad 49 percent. William F. Goltra, "Comparative Cost of Ties and Lumber on New York Central Lines West of Buffalo during the Last Twenty Years," *Railway Storekeeper,* II (June 1909), 102–111, and graphs; also summarized in *Sixth Annual Meeting of the Railway Storekeepers' Association* (Chicago, 1909), 267–275. The Forest Service census of ties showed no increase of prices, 1907–1909, except for small quantities of gum and spruce.

2. U.S. Department of Agriculture, Bureau of Forestry, *Annual Report of the Forester, 1904,* 182.

3. Gifford Pinchot, "A Federal Forest Service," *Proceedings of the American Forest Congress held at Washington, D.C., January 2 to 6, 1905,* under the auspices of the American Forestry Association (Washington, D.C.: Suter, 1905), 394.

4. Gifford Pinchot, comment on Question I–A, "Wooden Sleepers or Crossties," *Proceedings,* International Railway Congress Association, 7th session, Washington, D.C., May 1905, I (English ed., Brussels: P. Weissenbruch, 1906), 105.

5. Ernest Bruncken, "On the Course of Prices in Forestry," *Forestry Quarterly,* VI (Sept. 1908), 241.

6. Bruncken's fuller explanation of the course of prices in forestry demonstrates that it was possible to go beyond the Forest Service theory. His conception of demand was that of a modern economist, a function relating price to consumption. He believed the demand

for high-grade wood was strongly price elastic, a conception not apparent in current Forest Service publications. "Instead of a world market," he argued, "there are for wood a number of market districts . . ." The greatest local variations in prices, he said, occur among districts where uses for a species are simple and the markets narrow, as with firewood. The smallest variation occurs in the large wood markets for diverse industrial uses. Bruncken attributed the recent price increase in part to speculation and monopoly. He recognized, "In various ways, the price of every other article of human consumption reacts upon forest products," and he described several kinds of substitution. "If the kind of wood ordinarily used becomes too expensive, the consumer is often at liberty either to take the next poorer quality, or to employ an entirely different kind of wood, or finally, to dispense with wood altogether and substitute some other material. This is one of the forces tending to keep wood prices within reasonable limits, notwithstanding the circumscribed area from which ordinarily supplies may be drawn . . . Often a very small increase in price will bring the next best species into competition, *ibid.*, 243–244, 251.

7. William L. Hall, "The Waning Hardwood Supply and the Appalachian Forests," U.S. Department of Agriculture, Forest Service, *Circular* (No. 116, 1907), 14, 9.

8. Raphael Zon, "The Future Use of Land in the United States," *ibid.* (No. 159, 1909), and "Management of Second Growth in the Southern Appalachians," *ibid.* (No. 118, 1908).

9. See U.S. Department of Agriculture, *Annual Report of the Forester,* 1899, 1900, 1901, for discussion of budgets and mailing lists.

10. U.S. Department of Agriculture, *Annual Report of the Forester, 1901,* 325.

11. The largest was at Purdue University, Lafayette, Indiana, under W. K. Hatt. Others were in New Haven (J. W. Toumey and H. D. Tiemann); Berkeley (L. E. Hunt); St. Louis; Charleston, South Carolina; Eugene, Oregon; Boulder, Colorado; Moscow, Idaho; and Seattle (Rolf Thelen). Most were associated with universities, in forestry or engineering schools. James Cronin, *Hermann von Schrenk, The Man Who Was Timber* (Chicago: Kuehn, 1959),

describes the vicissitudes of the Mississippi Valley Laboratory at St. Louis, a "cooperative" effort of the Bureau of Plant Industry and the Bureau of Forestry.

12. William L. Hall of the Forest Service requested and obtained the cooperation of the American Railway Engineering Association. *Proceedings,* American Railway Engineering Association, VII (1906). F. E. Turneaure was the chairman of the AREA Impact Tests program. The choice of a location is discussed in Charles A. Nelson, "A History of the Forest Products Laboratory," unpub. diss., University of Wisconsin, 1964. See also U.S. Department of Agriculture, Forest Service, Forest Products Laboratory, Historical Correspondence on Establishment of Forest Products Laboratory at Madison, Wisconsin, ed. Donald G. Coleman (duplicated, RPI–75, Jan. 1960).

13. *Proceedings,* American Railway Engineering Association, II (1901), 104.

14. *Ibid.,* III (1902), 93.

15. *Ibid.,* VII (1906), 30.

16. *Ibid.,* VIII (1907), 459.

17. Goltra, "Comparative Cost of Ties."

18. "Report on Crossties," by Maintenance of Way and Structures Committee, in *Altoona Railroad Club of the Pennsylvania Railroad* (No. 1, 1910).

19. A. F. Robinson, representing Santa Fe railroad, in *Proceedings,* American Railway Engineering Association, IX (1908), 304.

20. "Report of Committee on Conservation of Natural Resources," *ibid.,* XVI (Bulletin No. 174, 1915), 989.

21. J. W. Kendrick, Vice-President of Atchison, Topeka, and Santa Fe Railroad, address, *ibid.,* XI (1910), 581.

22. Charles F. Manderson, "What Information Is Most Urgently Needed by Railroads Regarding Timber Resources," *Proceedings of the American Forest Congress held at Washington, D.C., January 2 to 6, 1905;* also cited in U.S. Department of Agriculture, Bureau of Forestry, *Circular* (No. 33, 1905), 19.

23. The meeting was reviewed critically in *Forestry Quarterly,* VIII (Mar. 1910), 138. The Forest Service expressed willingness to cooperate and presented evidence that there was an actual railroad timber problem and costs of plantations (apparently as cited in note

18), but there was no "definite idea in the minds of those present as to what should be done." The radically different point of view of the service and the railroad men was apparent.

24. One exception was an address by R. S. Kellogg and E. A. Ziegler, "The Cost of Growing Timber," Address to the 7th Annual Meeting of the National Lumber Manufacturers Association, 1909 (published separately by *The American Lumberman* [1911]). The authors claimed that growing white pine in New England should be profitable, loblolly pine would pay if prices rose a little, and slow-growing longleaf pine and red oak could not be grown profitably "unless we favor it." It might be possible to get more than 4 percent from Douglas fir since the price of stumpage was "certain to advance." Cutover, they argued, was an excellent investment, but became unreasonable when high rates of interest were "demanded." That is, a strongly biased presentation of the profitability of forestry was based upon assumptions of modest interest rates and rising prices.

25. "News and Notes," *American Forestry,* XVI (July 1910), 445; see also comments of C. F. W. Felt, *Proceedings,* American Railway Engineering Association, XVI (1915), 992.

26. The principal sources of data on Pennsylvania experiments are manuscript files in the office of the Forester, Pennsylvania Railroad, Philadelphia, notably an advisory report of R. C. Bryant, "A Forest Policy Recommended for the Pennsylvania Railroad Lines East of Pittsburgh and Erie," 1906. Before World War I numerous items were published on these projects in *Forestry Quarterly* and *Forest Leaves.* The management experiment is described by John Foley, "Forestry of a Railroad," *Forest Leaves,* XV (Apr. 1912), 119. Other published sources are *Proceedings,* American Railway Engineering Association, XVI (1915); R. C. Bryant, "Railroad Forest Plantations, Some Mistakes Made in Establishing Them," *Forestry Quarterly,* V (No. 1, 1907), 20; John Foley, "The Work of the Foresters of the Pennsylvania Railroad System," *Journal of Forestry,* XXII (1924), 162.

27. For a general discussion of the Adirondack Park history and the interests involved, see Roger C. Thompson, "Politics in the Wilderness: New York's Adirondack Forest Preserve," *Forest*

History, VI (No. 4, 1963), 14; see also Roger C. Thompson, "The Doctrine of Wilderness: A Study of the Policy and Politics of the Adirondack Preserve-Park," unpub. diss., State University of New York, College of Forestry, Syracuse, 1962.

28. Editorial, "Railroads in the Adirondacks," *Garden and Forest,* IV (June 10, 1891), 265; "Railroads and the Adirondack Reservation," *ibid.,* XII (July 10, 1899).

29. The D & H purchased the Chateaugay Ore and Iron Company and the Plattsburg-Lake Placid railroad. The Bureau of Forestry survey was conducted by Thomas H. Sherrard. The lumber was sold to the Dock and Coal Company of Plattsburg, and softwoods to Glen Falls Paper Mill Company. Lumbering ceased in 1919, and control of fires became possible thanks to the neighboring organization of the Adirondack Park. See *American Forestry,* XVII (May 1911), 313, or Ernest A. Sterling, "Forest Management on the Delaware and Hudson Adirondack Forest," *Journal of Forestry,* XXX (May 1932), 569–574.

30. "A Great Railroad's Interest in Forestry," *The Forester,* VII (Dec. 1901), 308–309. The meeting of November 22–23 at Cumberland, Maryland, was described as "the most interesting ever devoted to forestry in this country." Two hundred B & O railroad men were present. Von Schrenk and Pinchot were principal speakers. The Baltimore newspapers reported it. The Bureau of Forestry survey and working plan for the B & O tract are documented in the U.S. Department of Agriculture, Bureau of Forestry, *Annual Report of the Forester, 1903.* Other working plans and surveys of the bureau for private forest owners are listed in *Annual Reports of the Forester* for 1901, 1902, 1903.

31. James MacMartin, "Report of Committee on the Conservation of Natural Resources," *Proceedings,* American Railway Engineering Association, XVI (1915), 991.

32. *Ibid.*

Chapter 6

1. See, for example, A. J. McClatchie, "Eucalypts Cultivated in the United States," U.S. Department of Agriculture, Forest Service,

Bulletin (No. 35, 1902); William L. Hall and Hermann von Schrenk, "The Hardy Catalpa," *ibid.* (No. 37, 1902); "Eucalypts," *Circular* (No. 59, 1907); "Fence-post Trees," *ibid.* (No. 69, 1907); "Hardy Catalpa," *ibid.* (No. 82, 1907); R. S. Kellogg, "Forest Planting in Western Kansas," *ibid.* (No. 161, 1909). In earlier publications the fast-growing catalpa and osage orange were described as of growing economic importance. By about 1910 statements were tempered: "Forest Service statements have been abused, extravagant estimates of the probable returns from planted eucalyptus have been widely circulated . . ." H. S. Betts and C. S. Smith, "Utilization of California Eucalypts," *ibid.* (No. 179, 1910).

2. See reports of the Committee on Conservation of Natural Resources, *Proceedings,* American Railway Engineering Association, X–XVI (1909–1915). The railroads played a defensive role in agitation for control of forest fires. They continued to cooperate with the Forest Products Laboratory on wood technology, as described below.

3. C. W. Tiffany, "Some Notes on Wood Preservation," *Forest Leaves,* XIII (Aug. 1910), 154.

4. Ernest A. Sterling, "Artificial Reproduction of Forests," *Forestry Quarterly,* VI (June 1908), 217.

5. Ernest A. Sterling, "Forestry for Railroads," *Proceedings,* Society of American Foresters, IV (No. 1, 1909), 38.

6. *Ibid.,* 35.

7. *Ibid.,* 37. Sterling also objected to the propaganda of "forest influences," the idea that forests were justified by the benefits of flood control or climate control. "As a result the forest engineer as a class is not considered fraternally by engineers in general."

8. Ernest A. Sterling, "Timber Supply in Relation to Wood Preservation," *Proceedings,* 7th Annual Meeting, American Wood-Preservers' Association (1911).

9. Ernest A. Sterling, "Wood Preservation as a Factor in Forest Conservation," *American Forestry,* XVIII (Oct. 1912), 627–634.

10. Ernest A. Sterling, "The Development and Status of the Wood Preserving Industry," *Scientific American Supplement* LXXVI (July 12, 1913), 24.

11. Ernest A. Sterling, "The Attitude of the Railroads towards Forest Fires," *Forest Leaves,* XVII (Feb. 1914).

12. Ernest A. Sterling, untitled comment, in *American Forestry,* XXI (June 1915), 731.

13. *Ibid.*

14. Hermann von Schrenk, "The Decay of Timber and Methods of Preventing It," U.S. Department of Agriculture, Bureau of Plant Industry, *Bulletin* (No. 14, 1902), 9, 66.

15. Hermann von Schrenk, "The Use of Timber by Railroads and Its Relation to Forestry," *Proceedings,* New York Railroad Club, XIII (1903), 180–196.

16. Hermann von Schrenk, "A General Consideration of Timber under Conditions of Modern Demand and Growth," *Proceedings,* New England Railroad Club (Feb. 1907), 10. Von Schrenk's attitude toward economic use and the role of scientific testing and his conception of the variability of wood closely resemble Fernow's. See U.S. Department of Agriculture, Bureau of Plant Industry, *Bulletin* (No. 14, 1902), and biographies of the two men, James A. Cronin, *Hermann von Schrenk, The Man Who Was Timber* (Chicago: Kuehn, 1959); Andrew Denny Rodgers III, *Bernhard Eduard Fernow, A Story of North American Forestry* (Princeton, N.J.: Princeton University Press, 1951).

17. Von Schrenk, W. K. Hatt, and three chemists operated a complete pilot wood-preserving plant "in the gulch." Chemicals and timber were donated by the Santa Fe, Burlington, and Frisco Railroads and by chemical manufacturers. Equipment was loaned by manufacturers. Salaries were paid by the Bureau of Forestry. Tests demonstrated the damage of steam processes to wood fibers and the importance of air seasoning wood before preservative treatment. A cheap open-tank method for treating fence posts was also developed. The American Wood Preservers Association convened for the first time, to observe these tests. The purpose of the cement tests was to standardize methods for sampling and testing cement and concrete. The fair also included a locomotive-testing plant, designed by the Pennsylvania. It was the fourth "and most perfect" in the nation. Locomotives were tested as a public spectacle, but with every precaution for scientific control of hundreds of variables.

18. The Edgemont plant was moved to Sheridan, Wyoming, because "Edgemont was too close to hell." The water supply was in-

adequate at Edgemont, and Sheridan was nearer the new construction sites and the sources of western yellow pine and Douglas fir. A second plant was built at Galesburg, Illinois, a point near the sources of hardwood supply and central to the Burlington system. The decision to try wood preserving in 1899 was influenced by the availability of western softwoods after the line was extended to meet the Northern Pacific at Billings, Montana, in 1894, by rising wood prices in the prairies, and by exceptionally large renewals which had to be made on the Burlington Lines built in the 1880s. The Northern Pacific and Great Northern jointly purchased the Burlington in 1901. The change of management provided opportunities for policy changes and encouraged the use of Douglas fir on the Burlington.

19. However, the Lowry and Rueping processes, developed in Europe and patented in the U.S. in 1906 and 1902, respectively, made it possible to recover some of the creosote by applying a vacuum. It was possible to achieve deeper penetration of the wood and still economize on creosote.

20. Report of Committee on Ties, *Proceedings,* American Railway Engineering Association, VII (1906), 31.

21. Botanists call these the black oak group (Section *Erythrobalanus*). Railroad terms are used here.

22. On the Pennsylvania, for example, untreated white oak ties lasted three or four years on six-degree curves, six or eight years in tangent track. The Burlington found that, without tie plates, on sharp curves, they would last only two years.

23. O. E. Selby, "A Study of the Stresses Existing in Track Superstructure and Rational Design Based Thereon," *Proceedings,* American Railway Engineering Association, VIII (1907), 52–59. About 1908 open-hearth steel was widely adopted for rail, on the Burlington among other lines. The new method of manufacture offered new opportunities for experimenting with the chemistry of steel.

24. The respective safety factors were 1.12 and 1.03 with no plates, and about 1.71 with plates. Maximum axle loads about 1910 were 62,000 on the Pennsylvania and 52,000 on the Burlington. Renewals were fewer on the PRR which had better ballast and a higher proportion of sidetrack. The average annual cost of tie renewals including labor was $275 and $327 per mile, respectively.

25. Reports of the Committee on Ties, *Proceedings,* American Railway Engineering Association, XVIII (1917) and XX (1919), contain tables reviewing the substitute tie experiments.

26. Prairie railroads expressed agreement, and their representatives dominated the committee. Report of Committee on Wood Bridges and Trestles, *ibid.,* XVII (1916).

27. Herbert M. Wilson, "Federal Investigations of Mine Accidents, Structural Materials and Fuels," *Transactions,* American Society of Civil Engineers, XXXIX (Paper No. 1171, 1910).

28. U.S. Department of the Interior, *Summary of Results Obtained in the Investigations under the Survey of Fuels and Structural Materials,* 59 Cong., 1 sess., 1906, Senate Doc. 214, 11.

29. The Pennsylvania Railroad built a mile of telegraph with octagonal reinforced concrete poles, east of Fort Wayne, Indiana. *Arboriculture,* V (Dec. 1906). In 1904 the Burlington began experiments on home-designed reinforced concrete ties, which were not a success. In 1911 the Burlington tested Universal steel ties, which they pronounced uneconomical in 1916 and removed in 1917.

30. McGarvey Cline and J. B. Knapp, "Properties and Uses of Douglas Fir," U.S. Department of Agriculture, Forest Service, *Bulletin* (No. 88, 1911), 48.

31. The Master Carbuilders, American Railway Master Mechanics (locomotive builders), and the AREA were associated with the effort to grade lumber. The AREA Committee on Wood Bridges and Trestles and Committee Q of the American Society for Testing Materials cooperated on specifications for structural timber. The Committee on Ties of the AREA proposed a tie specification in 1904, but disagreement as to a single ideal size prevented its adoption.

Chapter 7

1. Committee on Railway Labor, discussion, *Proceedings,* American Railway Engineering Association, XXII (1921).

2. The Forest Products Section of the U.S. Railroad Administration was criticized for its pricing policies. By building price

schedules without regard to freight rates, it appeared to favor expansion of production from distant areas such as Louisiana, Texas, Washington, and Oregon, contrary to the stated policy of expanding local production. The Railroad Administration failed to increase total production of ties or to alleviate the shortage. The Railroad Administration regarded the large tie contractors as unproductive middlemen. The contractors resented pricing policies that squeezed them, since they provided working capital to the small mills, marketing services, storage and seasoning, and some quality control. See "Report of a Special Committee Designated by President McCormick [of the Railway Tie Association] to Consider and Report on Mr. G. G. Yeomans' Article Appearing in 'Railway Review,'" *Cross Tie Bulletin,* III (Feb. 1922), 15–21. Yeomans' article, "Work of the Forest Products Section," is also reprinted, 21–25, as well as the editorial comment from *Railway Review,* 25–27.

3. A. R. Joyce (Joyce-Watkins Company), reported in *Proceedings,* Western Railway Club, XXXI (1918), 96.

4. In 1919 the Wood Preservation Committee of the AREA proposed a geographical zone in which zinc treatment was recommended during the "present scarcity." The idea was dropped after 1922. Experiments were performed with water gas tar and sodium fluoride during the crisis, but by the time enough interest was aroused, the shortage of creosote was over. Patent processes such as zinc meta-arsenate (ZMA) were also developed. About 1922 the railroads revived an interest in artificial seasoning to overcome the immediate shortages of seasoned material.

5. Analysis of papers and discussions of the American Railway Engineering Association corroborates this in all departments of railroads.

6. Hermann von Schrenk, "Selection and Proper Utilization of Lumber in Car Construction," *Proceedings,* Western Railway Club, XXXI (1918), 84–101.

7. E. E. Pershall, "Keeping up the Supply of Cross Ties," *Cross Tie Bulletin,* IX (Mar. 1928), 12.

8. *Ibid.,* 10–14.

9. In 1925 the Scott Tie Company of Detroit owned 100,000 acres of oak stumpage in Missouri and other tracts in Kentucky,

and it purchased 12,000 acres on the Duck and Buffalo rivers, in Tennessee.

10. Ernest A. Sterling, "Future Sources of Cross Tie Supply," *Railway Age,* LXXXII (No. 6, 1927), 429–430.

11. Pershall, "Keeping up the Supply of Cross Ties," 12.

12. Ahern and Pinchot attacked the Forest Service as well as the lumbermen for accepting waste elimination, a "palliative," instead of seeking a cure for devastation and depletion. George P. Ahern, *Deforested America* (Washington, D.C., 1928); see also Samuel Record, "Our Need for Knowledge of Tropical Timbers," *Transactions,* American Society of Mechanical Engineers, L (WDI-50-10, 1928), 13–19.

13. *Proceedings,* American Railway Engineering Association, XXVI (1925), 1033.

14. L. C. Collister, "Fiftieth Anniversary of the Santa Fe's Experiment with Eucalyptus," *Cross Tie Bulletin,* XXXIX (Feb. 1958), 9–10.

15. Letter of PRR forester, Paul Brentlinger to L. E. G., Apr. 19, 1955, MS file on Plantations, General Queries and Publicity, Office of the Forester, Pennsylvania Railroad, Philadelphia.

16. Ernest A. Sterling, "Forest Management on the Delaware and Hudson Adirondack Forest," *Journal of Forestry,* XXX (1932), 569–574.

17. J. H. Waterman, MS files on Catalpa, office of Superintendent of Timber Preservation, Burlington Lines, Galesburg, Illinois.

18. R. V. Reynolds and Albert H. Pierson, "Lumber Cut of the United States, 1870–1920," and "Declining Production and High Prices as Related to Forest Exhaustion," U.S. Department of Agriculture, Forest Service, *Bulletin* (No. 119, 1923), as cited in *Cross Tie Bulletin,* IV (June 1923), 6.

19. "Timber, Mine or Crop?" U.S. Department of Agriculture, *Yearbook, 1922,* 140.

20. "Timber Depletion, Lumber Prices, Lumber Exports, and Concentration of Timber Ownership" (June 1920), U.S. Department of Agriculture, Forest Service, *Report on Senate Resolution 311.* The report is popularly referred to as the Capper Report.

21. U.S. Department of Commerce and Labor, Bureau of Cor-

porations, Joseph E. Davies Commission, *The Lumber Industry* (Washington, D.C.: Government Printing Office, 1914), 36.

22. Rolf Thelen, "Substitution of Other Materials for Wood, Studies of the Lumber Industry," U.S. Department of Agriculture, Office of the Secretary, *Report* (No. 117, 1917).

23. *Ibid.,* 140.

24. "Annual Report of the Forester," U.S. Department of Agriculture, *Annual Reports, 1922,* 240.

25. Thelen, "Substitution of Other Materials for Wood," 74.

26. Aldo Leopold, "Forest Products Research and Profitable Forestry," *Journal of Forestry,* XXV (May 1927), 542, 548. Shortly after this article was published, Leopold was diverted to wildlife conservation and adopted an approach that was more aesthetic than economic.

27. *Ibid.,* 542, 543.

28. The Department of Commerce was created in 1903, was separated from the Department of Labor in 1913, and was reorganized in 1921 to concentrate on the two tasks described.

29. U.S. Department of Commerce, *Report to President's Agricultural Conference* (Washington, D.C.: Government Printing Office, 1925).

30. Standards were set for sizes of such things as paving bricks, files and rasps, bed blankets, and screw threads.

31. The conference was financed by an anonymous gift. Four hundred persons attended, including those concerned with wood preserving and the groups represented on the Central Committee on Lumber Standards. See "Proceedings, National Conference on Utilization of Forest Products, Washington, D.C., November 1924," U.S. Department of Agriculture, *Miscellaneous Circular* (No. 39, 1925). Active members of the National Committee on Wood Utilization included Forester William Greeley; Howard Andrews, representing the railway tie producers; and Richard Aishton, president of the Association of American Railroads.

32. National Committee on Wood Utilization, *Wood Construction,* ed. D. F. Holtman (New York: McGraw-Hill, 1929), preface. The National Lumber Manufacturers Association also received acknowledgment.

33. Wilson Compton, *Looking Ahead from Behind,* Address to 25th Annual Convention, Apr. 29, 1927 (Washington, D.C.: National Lumber Manufacturers Association, 1927).

34. The allied interests are apparent in the proposal of the Chamber of Commerce of the United States of America. See *Forest Research A National Undertaking* (Washington, D.C.: Chamber of Commerce of the United States of America, Natural Resources Department, 1927). Under the McSweeney-McNary Law annual outlays for forest research would triple or quadruple. Expenditures of the federal government would be about one-third of the total projected. Of that amount a third would be research conducted at the Forest Products Laboratory.

35. The letters were published in abridged form in *Cross Tie Bulletin,* IX (Mar. 1928), 20.

36. U.S. Department of Agriculture, Forest Service, *Report of the Forester, 1927,* 42.

37. U.S. Department of Agriculture, Forest Service, *Report of the Forester, 1929,* 1–3, 53.

Chapter 8

1. U.S. Department of Agriculture, Forest Service, *Report of the Forester, 1934,* 1.

2. U.S. Department of Agriculture, Forest Service, *Report of the Forester, 1935,* 47.

3. Frank J. Hallauer, in *A National Plan for American Forestry,* 73 Cong., 1 sess., 1933, Senate Doc. 12, I, 245. The director of the Forest Products Laboratory, Carlisle P. Winslow, wanted a forest economics division established at the laboratory. The Forest Service refused, but did put some economists on the Washington staff.

4. Joseph Eastman, statement of June 27, 1935, as cited in "Federal Coordinator's Comments on Cross Ties," *Cross Tie Bulletin,* XVI (Oct. 1935), 4.

5. Inman F. Eldredge, *The Forests and the Future of the South* (Washington, D.C.: Charles Lathrop Pack Forestry Foundation, 1947).

6. U.S. Department of Agriculture, Forest Service, *Report of the Chief of the Forest Service for the fiscal year ended June 30, 1937*, 1.

7. U.S. Department of Agriculture, Forest Service, *Report of the Chief of the Forest Service, 1938*, 2, 1, 4.

8. U.S. Department of Agriculture, Forest Service, *Report of the Chief of the Forest Service, 1939*, 1, 2, 5.

9. In 1939 the Railway Tie Association formed a conservation committee in strong reaction against the producers of pulp. In 1940 the RTA was willing to consider a Forest Service proposal for public control, but by 1941 they were satisfied that the pulp producers' activities were beneficial. *Proceedings,* American Railway Engineering Association, XLII (1941).

10. W. M. Oettmeier, "Conservation as Practiced on 208,000 Acre Forest," *Cross Tie Bulletin,* XVIII (Sept. 1937), 14–17.

11. Ernest A. Sterling, "Economic Relationship of Forestry and Industry," *Journal of Forestry,* XXXVI (Feb. 1938), 173–175, 177.

12. *Progress in Private Forestry* (Washington, D.C.: American Forest Products Industries, 1961), 5. The capital gains tax also influenced methods of bridge maintenance on the railroads. By repairing and replacing portions less than 51 percent of existing structures, and charging the repairs to operating costs, the railroads were using "62-cent dollars." The distinction favored piecemeal renewal, and therefore it favored the use of wood trestles rather than their replacement with concrete and steel structures.

13. Letter to author from David T. Mason, Jan. 15, 1970.

14. U.S. Office of Federal Co-ordinator of Transportation, "Report on Preservative Treatment of Railroad Ties" (Mimeo., Washington, D.C., 1936).

15. Untreated ties had been removed and replaced with treated ties. The average treated tie placed in the 1920s had not yet reached the end of its life; thus, there was a breathing spell during which fewer renewals were required.

16. Report of Committee on Ties, *Proceedings,* American Railway Engineering Association, XL (1939), 640.

17. "The Industry Speaks Regarding—Export Ties," *Cross Tie Bulletin,* XXIX (Apr. 1948), 12.

18. Joyce's statement is cited more fully in Chapter 7.

19. Research programs of the Association of American Railroads Engineering Division (American Railway Engineering Association) and the National Lumber Manufacturers Association are reviewed by G. M. Magee, "Research Potential for Treated Wood," *Cross Tie Bulletin,* XLII (Nov. 1961), 51–60. The budget for that research is reviewed, *ibid.* (Feb. 1961).

20. For example, the Timber War Production Project was organized in August 1943 by the Forest Service and the War Production Board, to assist in increasing production from small mills, especially in the Ozarks. The Lake States Experiment Station also did cost analyses for small mills. See, for example, C. J. Telford, "Operating Small Sawmills in Wartime," U.S. Department of Agriculture, Forest Service, Forest Products Laboratory, *Miscellaneous Publication* (No. 509, 1943). Cost analyses and innovations in operations of small mills are reported throughout *Cross Tie Bulletin* of 1943 and 1944.

21. Carlisle P. Winslow, "Wood Research Pays High Dividends," address of January 1945; George M. Hunt, "Forest Products Research in the United States in War and Peace," address to British Empire Forestry Conference, June 1947 (informal publications, mimeo. in library of Forest Products Laboratory, Madison, Wis.).

22. Wilson Compton, "Private Enterprise Better Than Nationalization of Forestry," *Cross Tie Bulletin,* XXV (Feb. 1944), 12, 14.

Chapter 9

1. R. E. Marsh, in *A National Plan for American Forestry,* 73 Cong., 1 sess., 1933, Senate Doc. 12, I, 124; see also "Timber Trends in the United States," U.S. Department of Agriculture, Forest Service, *Forest Resource Report* (No. 17, 1965), 77.

2. R. S. Kellogg and E. A. Ziegler, "The Cost of Growing Timber, Address to the 7th Annual Meeting of the National Lumber Manufacturers Association, 1909" (published separately by *The American Lumberman* [1911]).

3. Jacob Schmookler, *Invention and Economic Growth* (Cambridge, Mass.: Harvard University Press, 1966), Chapter 5, p. 202.

4. The method of applying sustained yield principles on National Forest working circles is discussed by Walter J. Mead, *Competition and Oligopsony in the Douglas Fir Lumber Industry* (Berkeley: University of California Press, 1966).

5. The use of "material balance" equations in resource analysis is widespread. See David Granick's comments in *Comparisons of the United States and Soviet Economies,* 86 Cong., 1 sess., 1959, Joint Committee Print, Pt. 1, 162.

6. One of the first comprehensive treatments of water as an economic good is the text by Jack Hirshleifer, James C. DeHaven, and Jerome Milliman, *Water Supply: Economics, Technology and Policy* (Chicago: University of Chicago Press, 1960).

7. The Temporary National Economic Committee sought to predict the impact of mechanization on employment. See the recent studies of Edwin Mansfield, *The Economics of Technical Change* (New York: Norton, 1968), and *Industrial Research and Technological Innovation* (New York: Norton, 1968).

8. The forest industries may be compared with steel, petroleum, or building materials such as glass and clay products. The importance of growing demand has been suggested for those industries in Peter Temin, *Iron and Steel in Nineteenth-Century America, An Economic Inquiry* (Cambridge, Mass.: M.I.T. Press, 1964); John L. Enos, *Petroleum Progress and Profits, A History of Process Innovation* (Cambridge, Mass.: M.I.T. Press, 1962); Marian Bowley, *Innovations in Building Materials, an Economic Study* (London: Duckworth, 1960).

Index

Index

Index

Index